SONG OF SONGS

The Bible is more than history and more than wisdom literature. It is a library of the emotions of the human soul.

• The yearning for spiritual love reaches its finest expression of eroticism in the *Song of Songs* which unites the innocence of flesh with the freshness of idealistic youth.

• The *Book of Ruth* is perhaps the greatest short story ever told – an agricultural idyllic romance proving that national identities need not be obstacles to the love of individuals, even between a woman and her mother-in-law. An outcast Moabitess Ruth wins over the heart of powerful Boaz and becomes grandmother to King David.

• *Lamentations* reveals the heartbreak of a prophet over the ultimate disaster of his people – the destruction of the Temple and of Jerusalem.

• *Ecclesiastes* is a philosophical treatise bordering on cynicism but still offers hope that, amidst the vanities and tears, youth, love, companionship and wisdom can still bring joy to human life.

• *Esther* is a fantasy comedy giving comfort to a victimised people who are able to turn the tables on their arch-enemy Haman through the beauty and subtlety of their own Queen Esther under the guidance of her cousin Mordecai.

In this interpretative translation, the variety and scope of the Bible comes to life and proves why it can give pleasure even to non-believing lovers of great literature.

SIDNEY BRICHTO *is a leading Liberal Jewish Rabbi and theologian who writes and lectures on Jewish, religious and moral issues.*

The People's Bible

Song of Songs

with The Book of Ruth, Lamentations,
Ecclesiastes *and* The Book of Esther

newly translated by Sidney Brichto

Sinclair-Stevenson

First published in Great Britain by
Sinclair-Stevenson
3 South Terrace, London SW7 2TB

British Library Cataloguing in Publication Data.
A CIP catalogue record for this book is available from
The British Library.

ISBN 0 953 73982 1

Typeset by Rowland Phototypesetting Ltd, Bury St Edmunds, Suffolk.
Printed and bound by Mackays of Chatham plc. Kent.

This new interpretative translation is dedicated to the memory of my brother, Chanan Herbert Brichto. He loved the Bible with enormous passion not for its historical veracity but for its moral and literary genius. His seminal books Towards a Grammar of Political Poetics *and* The Names of God *will, I am convinced, in time revolutionize biblical scholarship. His respect, bordering on worship, of those geniuses who were the vehicles of the 'Still Small Voice' of God, is what inspired me to make this attempt to give the Bible back to people of great, little, or no faith.*

I want to thank Christopher Sinclair-Stevenson whose faith in the project never wavered when my own began to ebb. This attempt is as much his creation as mine. I thank Beverley Taylor, my personal assistant for so many years, for her dedication and help in enabling me to fulfil my creative interests; and to my wife and children for their advice and patience in my pursuit of this ambitious project. Finally, to John Porter my own and Christopher's gratitude, for without his vision this Genesis and the accompanying volumes might never have seen the light of day.

SIDNEY BRICHTO

Preface

The simple purpose of this new Bible is to give it back to the people who welcome a good story, fine poetry, and inspiration. For too long now, the Bible has become the best-seller least read. There are several reasons for this, foremost among them the claim of believers that the Bible was written or inspired by God. As our age becomes increasingly secular such a claim has turned people away. Also, atheists and humanists maintain that the Bible is a pack of distortions and false prophecies which prevent men and women from accepting their full responsibility for human destiny.

Literate people, however, aware of the Bible as a great classic, feel obligated to read it. Most do not get very far. Repetitions, lack of chronological order, tedious genealogical inserts, stories which cry out for ecplanations which are not given, incomprehensible thoughts – all these elements, as well as the formal divisions into chapters and verses, have forced most readers to give up even before they have reached the middle of the first book of Genesis.

The purpose of this edition of the Bible is to recast it in such a manner as to make it readable. It will be the complete biblical text faithfully translated after reference to other translations. The biblical narrative style is so sparse that it leaves much to the imagination. This provides a challenge to consider what the author has left out. On occasion, the translator will respond by interacting with the text to fill out the story. To avoid confusion, such elaborations will be indicated by a different print font. This is done with the expectation that some readers will feel that they (and indeed they may be right) could have done better. Such reactions are welcome and proof that the editor's objective of making the Bible come alive has been achieved. Material which appears irrelevant and interrupts the flow is moved into an appendix. Words and sentences will be added, also in a different print font, when necessary to provide continuity and to remove seeming contradictions. References will abound, to enable the reader to find the place in a traditional Bible should he or she wish to make comparisons.

Since the Bible is a library of books, each book or group of books will therefore require special treatment, with a specific introduction to explain how the editor has dealt with the material in his attempt to enable you not only to possess a Bible but to read it with comprehension and even with pleasure.

The Name of God

The name of God as it appears in the Bible is YHVH (Hebrew script has no vowels). This is the ineffable name which was always read as Adonai, meaning 'my Lord'. The traditional translation of YHVH is therefore Lord. The Jerusalem Bible translation refers to God as Yahweh which most scholars believe was the pronunciation of the four consonants. I was tempted to follow this example, because the name makes God into a vital personality – the real hero of *Genesis*: creator, monitor and judge of humanity – rather than an abstract force. Cautious respect for tradition made me hold to 'the Lord', but I hope that the reader will remember that the Lord, the God of Israel, is portrayed as a personality revealing the full range of emotions; paternal justice, maternal compassion, love and reason, regret and anger, punishing and forgiving.

Song of Songs

Introduction

Is the physical act of love degrading? Would it be better if men and women were free of the burning passion roused by their sexual nature? Should individuals try to suppress their sexual impulses, and failing in this try to restrain their passions; and be modest and reserved in love-making and in the expression of passionate feelings? Not according to *Song of Songs*. This book of love songs presents to the reader exquisite erotic poetry full of images and similes which stir and excite sexual desires and the longing for fulfilment.

Sex Not Evil

During times when good Christians believed that sexual intercourse was a necessary evil, a curse on man brought upon himself when Adam and Eve ate of the forbidden fruit; when it was the common view that men had the irresistible but unfortunate urge to assert themselves sexually and that it was the duty of women to submit willingly but without joy to their desires, *Song of Songs* protested that this was not so: that love and the physical expression of love, promised and fulfilled, was beautiful and elevating. This message was proclaimed by its contents long before the countless love manuals which sought and still seek to remove the sense of guilt which has been the burden of generations since Western society accepted the duality of human nature: the conflicting elements of body and soul, with the corollary that spirituality depends upon the ability to suppress bodily desires, especially the sex drive.

The attitude of *Song of Songs* is not inconsistent with the rest of the Old Testament, in which there is no prudishness or deprecation of the sexual urge. According to one account of creation, woman is not created so that man can have children but because "It is not good that man should be alone." In the Book of *Genesis* we are told that Isaac was only comforted for the loss of his mother after he had taken Rebecca into his tent, i.e. had consummated his marriage. There is no recorded disapproval of Tamar for playing the whore for her father-in-law, Judah, Jacob's son, in order to gain her rights. Indeed it is through this extramarital act that the child is born who is the ancestor of King David.

The Prophets of Judah and Israel, when they wish to point to the sins of the people against God, express this most vividly by comparing God to the betrayed husband and Israel to the adulterous woman. For them, the best way to understand the anguish of a broken relationship is through the analogy to sexual betrayal. Indeed, *Ecclesiastes*, the most pessimistic book in the Old Testament, while it considers wealth, position and even wisdom as vain, advises the reader to enjoy life with a woman he loves all the days of his life.

The Holy of Holies

However, the vividness of the sexual images is more striking in *Song of Songs* than in any other book. This led the ancient Rabbis who decided the contents of the Canon to ask whether *Song of Songs* was worthy of inclusion. The most renowned Sage, Akiba, concluded the discussion by declaring that "All the Writings were holy, but *Song of Songs* was the Holy of Holies", and that the whole world realized its supreme purpose only on the day when *Song of Songs* was given to Israel.

Allegorical Interpretations

The fact that, in Judaism, these love songs have been interpreted as a description of the love between God and Israel, and in Christianity as the love between Jesus and the Church, may point to the embarrassment caused to the religious hierarchies by the inclusion in the Bible of such a frank avowal of the love between a man and a woman. But it may just as well be considered as their belief in the prophetic view that only someone who understands the intensity of the emotional and physical love between man and woman can know the religious experience of man's relationship with God. Perhaps, only the person who knows how to give himself completely, body and soul, to another can worship God with his total being.

Was King Solomon the Author?

The authorship as well as the literary unity of the book is the subject of scholarly controversy. Traditionally, as the first verse suggests, the book is ascribed to Solomon the romantic king who, in addition to building the great Temple in Jerusalem, also cemented relations with neighbouring kings and chieftains by marrying their daughters. More than diplomacy may have been in his mind, as we are told in the Book of Kings that he had in his harem 700 concubines as well as 300 wives. According to Jewish tradition, he wrote the Songs during the freshness of youth, the Book of Proverbs in the wisdom of maturity, and the Book of Ecclesiastes in the despair of old age.

It is more likely that the authorship of the book was ascribed to King Solomon in order to win for it more readers. The statement in the Book of Kings that he wrote 3,000 proverbs and 1,005 songs would lend credibility to his authorship. The ascription of authorship to famous men was a common practice of the Hellenistic period and is the best indication of the approximate date the book was written.

A Drama or a Collection of Songs

Many scholars maintain that the book has no story sequence but is a collection of wedding songs. Certain manuscripts of the Septuagint, the Greek translation of the Hebrew Bible, divide the text into songs in which the singers were the bride, the bridegroom (sometimes referred to as King) and the chorus. Others see the book as an idyllic drama about a country girl from the village of Shullam who because of her beauty takes the King's fancy. She would rather stay at home with her shepherd lover, but her brothers see the benefit of a relationship with the King. She is brought to the harem. The ladies of the harem (the Daughters of Jerusalem – or the Chorus) are astounded by the stubbornness of the girl who rebukes the King in favour of her shepherd lover. They mock her and sing the King's praises. She persists in pining for her boyfriend until the King accepts defeat and permits her to return home. After interrupted meetings during the course of the story, she is finally reunited with her lover and is able to testify to the constancy and power of true love. While this interpretation requires some imaginative play with the verses and may not have been the author's intention, it provides a framework which makes it more accessible to a modern audience. In any event, the sensuality of the erotic messages overrides the literary structure one chooses to accept.

A word has to be said about some extraordinary poetic images. The modern reader would be offended by the comparison of a woman's nose to the Tower of Lebanon or her neck to the Tower of David. One needs to understand the mind of the poet/lover. He is seeking to convey the aura her presence instills in him. As John Donne compares the body of his mistress to the American Continent, with its hills and valleys, so is the beauty of Shulam for her lover like the lands of Judah and Israel and its bordering nations. She is *his* world and in her he sees every sight which has ever stirred in him the emotions of awe, wonder and worship.

The Daughters of Jerusalem – The King's Harem

Employing the plot just outlined, the first scene begins with the country girl among the harem ladies who are attempting to entice the King into choosing one of them for his night's pleasure. They do this by praising his talents in love-making. The girl, provoked by the taunts of the fair-complexioned city girls of the harem, defends herself. In those days exposure to the sun was avoided by the upper classes. Her brothers were angry with her perhaps because of her meetings with the shepherd, and forced her to neglect her beauty by making her work in the vineyard under the heat of the scorching sun. She expresses her longing for the shepherd and wonders where she might find him. She is jeered at and referred to sarcastically as "loveliest of women"; told "to follow in the tracks of her flocks" and to take her own "kids to graze close by the shepherds' tents".

In the next scene she is with the King who tries to win her love by promises of jewels which will add to her beauty. But, as the King sings her praise, the girl's heart goes out to her shepherd who is as alive for her, in spite of his absence, as a "sachet of myrrh lying between my breasts".

With the words "How beautiful you are, my love . . ." begins a remembered exchange of compliments between the boy and girl and references to the simplicity of their own rustic surroundings in contrast to the opulence of the King's court. The girl refers to herself modestly as a simple meadow flower; but the boy, unwilling to contradict his beloved, says that, if she is only a lily, the other girls are as thorns. She responds by comparing him to an apple tree in a forest which provides fruit. Passion weakens her and she requires refreshment to sustain her.

The scene returns to the harem. When they press her to love the King, she tells them that love cannot be forced. The refrain "I charge you, daughter of Jerusalem . . ." is repeated several times in the book. The King sends her home with the hope that she may reconsider.

Her Lover Returns

The next act begins in her home where she is forbidden by her brothers from seeing the shepherd. She feels he is running to her as quickly as he can. With the grace of youth, he is "like a gazelle, like a young hart". He appears to tell her that spring has come and that it is time for lovers to be united. Frustrated by her brothers' watchfulness, he laments that she is hidden away as if in "the clefts of a rock". Since he cannot touch her, he asks to see her lovely face and to hear her sweet voice. She sings a song about little foxes which may allude to her brothers who are preventing their love from finding fulfilment. She affirms their love and suggests they meet under the protection of night. When he does not come, her longing is so great that she searches for him. She finds him, takes hold of him and brings him to the bedroom where she herself was conceived.

In the next scene the King comes to the girl's village to arrange the betrothal. All the villagers are amazed at the splendour of the King's entourage. The King seeks to win her love by the eloquence of his praise for her beauty. Her simple beauty does not make her any less regal in bearing. He is awed by her as one is by the sight of the majestic Tower of David. He takes her to his summer house in the Lebanon.

The Lovers Find Fulfilment

The shepherd has found her there and pleads: "Come from Lebanon, my promised bride". In the love poems which follow we hear the beauty of sensual love expressed in a manner without equal in any literature. For the boy, his beloved is more than his promised bride: she is like a sister one has known since childhood with whom one has shared all the experiences of growing up. His love is so great that the tiny area of flesh which surrounds one pearl of her necklace leaves him breathless. She possesses in her all the promise of pleasure, of smell, of taste and of touch. She is the paradise which is still locked to him, the fountain of waters from which he cannot drink. The girl is stirred by the extent of his love and opens herself to him and commands him to enter so that he may arouse and bring to fulfilment the pleasures contained in her. They make love.

As often happens, one dreams of disappointment and failure not before an expected event or test, but afterwards. So it is with the country girl who dreams that her lover has knocked and sought entrance into her room. She is at first coy about admitting him and, when she leaves her bed to do so, he is gone. She searches for him and in the dream is punished by the watchmen who beat her and reveal her nakedness, an expression perhaps of her guilt for having given herself to her beloved without her brothers' approval.

The ladies of the harem begin to be impressed by the sincerity of the girl's love and try to discover its reasons. She gives an ecstatic description of him. The harem is won over and is even prepared to assist in finding her lover. She tells them that he must be in his usual place, in "his garden ... the beds of spices ... pasturing his flocks among the lilies."

The King enters the harem and praises her in regal fashion comparing her effect upon him to the effect caused by an army in full and glittering military array. The King enveloped, by a bevy of beauties, "sixty queens, eighty concubines and countless maidens", sees the Shulammite girl as a unique creature. "But my dove is unique, mine, unique and perfect." When he leaves her, she explains how she was first seen by the King, "I went down to the nut orchard."

The King makes his last attempt to win the girl's heart. He pleads with her not to depart and sings again her praises, imagining the delights he thought would be his: "I will climb the palm tree, I resolved I will seize its clusters of dates." But to no avail, for she affirms again, "I am my beloved's and his desire is for me."

The Final Reunion

She is given permission to leave the palace, meets her lover and promises him all the pleasures of love she has saved for him once they return to the natural surroundings which they cherish. "Then I shall give you the gift of my love ... The mandrakes yield their fragrance, the rarest fruits are at our doors; the new as well as the old. I have stored them for you, my Beloved." She expresses that wish that he were her brother, so that she could show him her love without incurring disapproving eyes.

The girl and boy are seen by the villagers as they return home. They pass an apple tree which has special meaning for them as under it she was born and it was the place where he once awakened her from her sleep. The fervour of the lovers' desire is then expressed and with it the affirmation that there is no power greater, no force more terrible than love: "For love is strong as death."

ACT ONE 1:1-4

Scene 1

In the Chambers of the Harem

THE DAUGHTERS OF JERUSALEM

(Praising the King in the presence of the girl from the Village of Shulam who has been brought to the harem because she took his fancy.)

O for the kisses of his mouth
For your caresses are more intoxicating than wine
The smell of your fragrance is delightful
Like the smoothness of oil your name trips **off our tongue**
No wonder the young girls adore you.

Take me
Let us run . . .
The King has brought me into his chambers
We will revel in joy
Our love-making will be more memorable than wine
So deeply do we love you.

THE SHULAMMITE

(While changing to meet the King, the Daughters of Jerusalem make fun of her dark complexion.)

Yes, I am darkened **by the sun**
Yet I am lovely
Like the tents of **the men of** Keder,
But also, like **the colours of** the curtains of Solomon.
Do not look at me **with disdain** because I am black.
It is the sun that has tanned me,
Because my brothers were angry
And made me to keep their vineyards, so that
My own vineyard, I did not keep.

(She expresses her yearning for her shepherd lover)
Tell me, O love of my heart,
Where do you pasture at mid-day
And rest your flock?
For I do not want to cover my face
When I wander around
The flocks of your fellow **shepherds.**

THE DAUGHTERS OF JERUSALEM *(with sarcasm)*
If you do not know, you **who are** the loveliest of women,
Follow in the tracks of the herds,
And feed your own goats where the shepherds dwell.

Scene 2

The King's Banqueting Hall

THE KING
To me, my love, you are graceful
Like a filly in the chariots of Pharaoh.
How adorable are your cheeks,
With **your** plaits of hair **touching them,**
And your neck **which peeps** out of its string of beads.
But, we shall make for you necklaces of gold
Studded with silver.

THE SHULAMMITE *(To herself)*
Even while the King lies on his couch
My spikenard gushed forth its fragrance to the King.
Ah, but **the head** of my beloved is like a sachet of myrrh
Lying between my breasts.
Yes, my beloved is like a cluster of henna blossoms
Which climb up the vines of En-gedi

(The Shulammite remembers her lover's praise and her responses)

– How beautiful you are, my love,
How beautiful you are
Your eyes are as doves
So pure and innocent.

– *No*, it is you my beloved who are beautiful
And so full of delight
Our bed is a green meadow,
The roof beams of our house cedar
And its panels cypresses.

– I am only a blossom out of Sharon
A wild lily of the valleys.

– *But*, as a lily among thorns
So is my love among women.

– As an apple tree in the forest
So is my love among men.
I delighted to dwell under its shadow
And his fruit was sweet.
He took me to the inn
And his love hovered over me like a banner.
Sustain me with draughts of wine
Revive me with the smell of apples
For I swoon with love.
I let his left hand support my head
As his right hand embraces me.

CHORUS

I implore you. O daughters of Jerusalem.
By the gazelles and by the hinds of the fields,
Not to try to awaken nor stir up love,
Until it pleases.

ACT TWO

Scene 1

(The King's advances being spurned, he allows the Shulammite to return home and to reconsider his proposal to make her one of his wives.)

The Shulammite in her home under the guardianship of her brothers

THE SHULAMMITE *(Hears her lover's approach)*
>I hear the sound of my beloved,
>He is coming!
>Skipping over the hills,
>For my beloved is like a deer or a young hart.
>Now, he stands by my wall
>He is looking through the windows
>And shows himself through the lattice.
>My beloved spoke. [He said to me:]

THE SHEPHERD
>"Rise up my love, my beautiful one,
>And come,
>Winter has ended
>The rain is over and gone.
>Flowers are peeping through the ground
>The time of singing is come.
>And the cooing of the turtle-dove can be heard in our
>   land
>The fig tree is ripening with her first figs
>The vines are blossoming
>And giving forth their smell.
>Up, my love, my lovely one

Come away.
My dove, hidden in the clefts of the rocks
In the coverts of the cliff
Let me see your face
Let me hear your voice.
For your voice is sweet
And your face is beautiful."

THE SHULAMMITE
"Save us from the foxes
The little foxes that spoil the vineyards
When our vineyards are in blossom.
My beloved is mine and
I am his,
He who pastures his flock among the lilies
Until the day breathes with the breezes of dawn
And the shadows flee away.
Return **to me**
Be like a gazelle,
A young hart,
Upon the mountains of spices.

Scene 2

The Shulammite recalls her dream

THE SHULAMMITE
By night, on my bed
I looked for him who is the love of my life
I looked for him but could not find him
I said, I will get up and go to the town centre
In the streets and the village squares
I will look for the love of my life
I looked but did not find him.

But the watchmen guarding the town found me.
    I said to them: "Have you seen the love of my life?"
Soon after I left them
    I found the love of my life
    I held him fast and would not let him go.
Until I brought him into my mother's house
    And into the room of her who gave me birth.

CHORUS
    I implore you, O daughters of Jerusalem,
    By the gazelles and by the hinds of the field,
    Not to try to awaken nor stir up love,
    Until it pleases.

ACT THREE   3:6–11

Scene 1

The King approaches the village of the Shulammite once again to win the young girl's heart

THE TOWNSFOLK

What is this coming up from the country
Like a column of smoke
Giving off vapours of myrrh and frankincense
And every known perfume?

Look, it is Solomon's procession
Surrounded by sixty warriors
Of the champions of Israel.
All master swordsmen
And skilled in war
Each man with sword at his thigh.
Against ambushes by night.

CHORUS

King Solomon had made for him a regal tent
    Of wood from Lebanon
He ordered its posts to be made of silver,
    The roof of gold
The seat purple
    Its linings embroidered with words of love
From the Daughters of Jerusalem
Go out, O Daughters of Zion, and look at King Solomon
Wearing the crown with which his mother crowned him
On his wedding day,
    The day of his heart's delight.

THE KING *(Wooing the Shulammite)*
> O, so beautiful you are, my love, so beautiful
> Your eyes appear as doves behind your veil.
> Your hair like a flock of goats
> That wend their way down from Mount Gilead.
> Your teeth are like a flock of ewes
> All shaped to perfection,
> Coming up washed **by the spring**.
> All are paired and none is missing.
>
> Your lips are like threads of scarlet,
> And the sound of your voice is captivating
> Behind your veil,
> Your cheeks are like a pomegranate split in half...
>
> Your neck is like the Tower of David,
> A fortress arrayed with a thousand shields
> And the dazzling armour of warriors.
> Your two breasts are two fawns
> Twins of a gazelle
> Which pastures among the lilies.

THE SHULAMMITE *(Excusing herself)*
> Until the day breathes with the breezes of dawn
> And the shadows flee away
> I will go to the mountain of myrrh,
> And to the hill of frankincense.

Scene 2

**The King's summer house in the Lebanon
to which the Shulammite has been taken**

(The shepherd lover finds her there)

THE SHEPHERD
> You are perfect in beauty
> And there is not a blemish on you.

Come with me from Lebanon, my bride,
Come with me from Lebanon.
Come down from the top of Amana
From the heights of Senir and Hermon
From the dens of lions
From the mountains where leopards roam.
You have ravished my heart, my sister, my bride,
You have ravished my heart
With one glance from your eyes
With one bead of your necklace.
How wonderful are your caresses, my sister, my bride!
How much better are your caresses than **flagons of** wine,
And the smell of your body than all manner of spices.
Your lips drop honey, O my bride,
I taste honey and milk under your tongue
The scent of your clothes is like the scent of Lebanon.

*(They leave the confines of the King's summer house to find a
meadow where they sit down)*

THE SHEPHERD

A garden locked up is my sister, my bride,
A spring sealed, a fountain secured.
Your body gives off the fragrances of an orchard of
　　pomegranates
With **smells of** precious fruits, **that of**
Henna and spikenard plants,
Yes, spikenard as well as saffron, calamus and
　　cinnamon
With all trees of frankincense,
Myrrh and aloes
With all the rare spices.
You are a fountain of gardens
A well of living waters
And flowing streams from Lebanon.

THE SHULAMMITE

> Awake, O north wind,
> And come, wind of the south,
> Blow upon my garden
> That its smells may flow out.
> Let my beloved
> Enter into his garden
> And taste his precious fruits.

THE SHEPHERD

> Ah, I have entered into my garden,
> My sister, my bride.
> I have gathered my myrrh with my spices
> I have eaten my honey and my honeycomb
> I have drunk my wine with my milk.

CHORUS

> *Eat, O friends,*
> *Drink, drink deeply*
> *All you lovers!*

Scene 3

> *The Shulammite returns to the king's summer house. In her*
> *sleep she has an anxiety dream which she tells to the*
> *members of the harem – the Daughters of Jerusalem.*

THE SHULAMMITE

> I sleep but my heart is awake
> The voice of my beloved
> He knocks **at the door:**
> "Open it for me
> My sister, my bride,
> My dove, my perfect one, for
> My head is covered with dew
> My hair with drops of the night."

But I have taken off my dress
How shall I dress again?
I have already washed my feet.
Shall I make them dirty?
My beloved put in his hand through the hole in the door.
My stomach turned over because of him.
I rose to open to my beloved -
My hands moist with myrrh
My fingers dripping myrrh
On the handles of the lock.
I opened for my beloved
But my loved one had turned back.
He was gone.
The sound of him made me feel faint.
I looked for him, but could not find him.
I cried out for him, but he did not answer me.

The guards that patrol the town found me.
They struck me.
They hurt me.
The guardians of the wall stole my coat.
I beseech you, O Daughters of Jerusalem,
If you should find my beloved.
What should you tell him?
Tell him that I am lovesick.

THE DAUGHTERS OF JERUSALEM
What makes your beloved more than other beloveds,
O you, most beautiful among women?
What makes your beloved more than other beloveds
That you implore us so?

THE SHULAMMITE
My beloved is young and ruddy
One in ten thousand.
His head is a crown of precious stones.

The curls of his hair are black as a raven.
His eyes are **pure** like doves by brooks of water
Washed in milk, perfectly set.
His cheeks are like beds of spices,
Hillocks of sweet herbs,
His lips like lilies
Moist with flowing myrrh.
His fingers are like rods of gold
With nails made of **pink** beryl.
His body is like polished ivory
Overlaid with sapphires.
His legs are like marble columns
Set upon feet of pure gold.
His presence is like the Lebanon
Majestic as its cedars.
His mouth is sweet.
Yes, he is altogether lovely.
This is my beloved, and this is my darling,
O Daughters of Jerusalem.

DAUGHTERS OF JERUSALEM
Impressed by her description of him.
Where has your beloved gone,
O you most beautiful of women?
Where has your beloved turned?
We will seek him with you.

THE SHULAMMITE
My beloved has gone down to his garden
To the beds of spices
To feed in the gardens
And to gather lilies.

I am my beloved's
And my beloved is mine:
He pastures his flocks among the lilies.

The King enters the harem and addresses the Shulammite.

KING

You are beautiful, my love, as Tirzah,
As delightful as Jerusalem.
Awesome as an army **parading** under banners.
Turn away **your face** from me
For **a look from** your eyes overwhelms me.
Your **flowing** curls are like a flock of goats,
Trailing down from Mount Gilead.

(He repeats his earlier praises of her.)
Your teeth are like a flock of ewes,
Coming up washed from the water springs.
All are paired and none is missing.
Behind your veil,
Your cheeks are like a pomegranate split in half.

There are **for me** sixty queens
And eighty concubines
And countless young women
But you, my dove, are unique,
You are my perfection.
Just as you are unique to your mother;
Her very favourite.
Women who look upon her
Think her most favoured.
Yes, queens and concubines praise her:
"Who is she that appears as the dawn
Seductive as the moon
Radiant as the sun.
Awesome as an army parading under banners?"

THE SHULAMMITE

Reflecting aloud on how she innocently came to the attention of the King
To the nut garden, I went down,

To look at the new plants of the valley,
To see if the vines were budding,
And the pomegranates in flower.
Before I knew it
My life was **totally changed.**
I was placed in the carriages of the royal entourage.

(She pleads to leave the Court.)

KING

Return, do not go away, Shulammite girl.
Return, return, so that we may look at you **again.**

THE SHULAMMITE *Amazed by his attention*

What do you see in this girl from Shulam?
I am not a dance between two chorus lines.

(The King's final attempt to win her heart)

THE KING

How **beautiful are** your feet in sandals,
You who could be a prince's daughter.
The curvature of your thighs
Moves as gracefully as links of a necklace,
The work of a master artisan.
Your navel is a well rounded goblet,
With no lack of vintage wine.
Your belly is like a bundle of wheat
Encircled by lilies.

*   *   *

Your two breasts are two fawns, twins of a gazelle.
Your neck is a tower made of ivory.
Your eyes are like the pools of Heshbon
By the gate of Bath-rabbin.
Your nose is like the tower of Lebanon,
Seen **at a distance** from Damascus.

*   *   *

Your head is as majestic as Mount Carmel
And your hair's colour is like royal purple.
The King is captivated by its tresses.
How beautiful, how charming, **my** love
You are the source of **my** delight.

*   *   *

Your stature is like a palm tree
Your breasts like clusters of grapes.
I said: "I will climb that palm
I will take hold of its boughs."
Let your breasts be clusters of grapes
And your breath as sweet as apples.
Your mouth is like good wine
Flowing so smoothly for the beloved,
Gliding through the lips of those that are as asleep.

The Shulammite: **No**, I am my beloved's
And his yearning is for me alone.

ACT FOUR 7:12–14

*(The King has relented, appreciates that he has many wives
and concubines and that the Shulammite maiden would be
exclusively her lover's. He gives the couple his blessing. They
return home.)*

Scene 1

Outside the King's summer palace

THE SHULAMMITE

Come my beloved,
Let us go through the fields
We will lodge in the villages.
We will get up early and go down to the vineyards
To see if the vines are budding
Whether their blossoms are opening,
If the pomegranates are in flower.
There will I give you my love.

The mandrakes surrender their smell.
And at our doors are the choicest of fruits.
New and old
I have saved them for you.
O my beloved.

Scene 2

*(They approach their village hand in hand and are worried at
the disapproval she will receive from her brothers for rejecting
the King in favour of a shepherd.)*

THE SHULAMMITE

Oh, if only you were my brother,
Who sucked at my mother's breast.

Then if I chanced upon you in the street
I could kiss you
Without people despising me.
I would lead you
And bring you into my mother's house.
There you would teach me.
And I would give you spicy wine to drink
From the juice of my pomegranates.

His left hand supports my head
As his right hand embraces me.

CHORUS

I implore you, O Daughters of Jerusalem,
By the gazelles and by the hinds of the field,
Not to try to waken nor stir up love,
Until it pleases.

THE VILLAGERS

(Amongst themselves beyond earshot of the Shulammite and
her lover)
Who is this coming up from the country,
Leaning on her beloved?

THE SHULAMMITE

(Pointing to a tree where she once awoke him)
Under that apple tree I woke you,
The same tree where your mother was in labour with
     you.
There she was in labour and gave birth to you.

Set me as a seal upon your heart
As a seal upon your arm!
Declaring that love is as strong as death,
That jealousy is as cruel as the nether world.
Its flashes are flashes of fire
A very flame of The LORD.

THE SHEPHERD

> Floods of waters cannot quench *my* love
> Nor could rivers drown it.
> If a man were to offer all his wealth to obtain love,
> He would be ridiculed.

THE SHULAMMITE

> *(Later when the Shulammite has arrived home, she says to her friends.)*
> **"My brothers said:**
> We have a little sister,
> She has no breasts
> What shall we do for our sister
> In the day when she is courted?
>
> If she **is fortified like** a wall
> We will adorn her with silver trophies.
> But, if she be a door
> We will shut her in with boards of cedar.
>
> **I said to them:**
> I am a wall,
> But my breasts are like towers.
> Then was I in my beloved's eyes
> As one who brought contentment.

THE SHEPHERD *(Says to his friends)*

> Solomon has a vineyard at Baal-hamon,
> He leased it out to keepers.
> Everyone for the sale of the fruit
> Earned a thousand pieces of silver.
> My vineyard, which is mine, is before me.
> You, Solomon, can have a thousand.
> And those who are its keepers two hundred . . .

(The lover and friends appear at his beloved's home and he says to her)

THE SHEPHERD

O you, who dwells in the gardens,
My companions want to hear the sound of your voice.
Let me hear it.

THE SHULAMMITE

Make haste, my beloved,
And be like a gazelle or a young hart
Upon the mountains of spices . . .

The Book of Ruth

Introduction

The story of Ruth is unparalleled in its simplicity. It is a rustic epic of loyalty between two women which culminates in the birth of the greatest king of Israel, David. The author succeeds through the poetic brevity of the narrative to give readers a sense of being there; in creating for us the agrarian world of Judea at the time when the Judges ruled the Tribes of the twelve sons of Jacob, renamed Israel.

After the settlement of Israel's descendants in Canaan in c. 1200 BC, most towns within their tribal borders enjoyed virtual autonomy. The men of substance had the responsibility of keeping order in the town; they were called upon to give judgement on civil matters such as ownership of property, familial responsibilities, divorce and felonies like theft and adultery. Peer pressure and the importance of being respected, it is imagined, led them to act justly within the confines of a society divided between landowners and labourers. When the town was under threat from a foreign enemy, her men would join arms with other tribal villages to defend themselves. Occasionally, the entire tribe would accept as their war chief a charismatic individual who was able to unite them and defeat their enemies. One great victory was all that was needed to establish such an individual as *primus inter pares;* to make him worthy of gifts and the source for judgement when differences arose between the villages or the individuals within them. The Book of Judges should be read for a better appreciation of this period.

The story was written after the Judeans, under an edict of Cyrus in 536 BCE, returned to Jerusalem and Judea to re-establish themselves in their homeland. Some years after the initial return of the exiles, the histories of Ezra and Nehemiah record their disappointment with the early returnees who had married the native women and had forsaken the worship of The LORD, their ancestral God. During a dramatic day, Ezra read the entire Law of Moses to all the Judeans and persuaded all the men to expel their non-Jewish wives and their gods with them.

Against this background, the story of Ruth appears as a protest against this xenophobia, as the heroine is a Moabite woman, and Mosaic Law forbids any Moabite or Ammonite from entering into the sanctuary of The LORD, i.e. to be accepted as a member of the community. The reason for this stricture was the unfriendliness of the nations of Moab and Ammon towards the Israelites on their journey to the Promised Land. They were not given permission to pass through their borders and had to go the long way around. Better behaviour was expected of them as they were cousins (their ancestor was Lot, the nephew of Abraham, the first patriarch). Undoubtedly it was the ban on these two nations that led to the biblical besmirching of their ancestors. When Lot, his wife and two daughters escaped from the brimstone and fire which engulfed the twin cities of sin, Sodom and Gomorrah, Lot's wife turned into a pillar of salt for looking back. The two daughters were convinced that God had wiped out all the world's inhabitants and that only they remained alive. To continue the human race, they got their father drunk and on two successive nights slept with him. The consequence was two sons whom they named Moab, meaning "from my father", and Ben Ammi (Ammon), meaning "son of my people". Children born out of incest are according to Mosaic Law *mamzerim*, pariahs, who could not enter The LORD's sanctuary and could only marry other *mamzerim*. This curse was not limited to one generation but went on *ad infinitum*. The biblical author wishes us to know that the children of Lot in their unfraternal animosity towards the Israelites were fulfilling their perverse tendencies.

How extraordinary, therefore, that while Naomi's husband and two sons die prematurely, perhaps as a punishment for leaving Judea to live in a foreign land, a Moabitess is pictured in such a saintly fashion and is awarded the ancestry of King David. Was this a protest against Ezra's draconian expulsion of all the non-Jewish women or an indication that his measure only applied to women who worshipped other gods? Is it to exclude from the ban those Babylonian women who accompanied their Judean husbands who had returned with them? Saying as Ruth had to Naomi, "Your people are my people and your God is my God"?

Proof that Ruth's story is in the realms of fantasy and not history is the names given to the characters. Each name describes either their fate or personality. Ruth means *friendship*; Naomi, *sweetness*, turning into Marah, *bitterness*; the two sons are named *Disease* and *Withering away*. Ironically, fundamentalists will attack us for assuming that the tale is fictional when those who heard the story when it was first told would by virtue of these fictitious names know that the author was weaving a tale for both their enjoyment and edification.

The story is a literary gem. It hurls us back in time and stimulates us to imagine how life would have been for us had we been living then. The readers of the books of the settlement of Canaan – Joshua and Judges, even Samuel and Kings – will see that it was a cruel and ruthless age and not as idyllically drawn by the author. The story of Ruth is an oasis in a moral desert; a vision of halcyon days which was the objective of all the Jewish Prophets: the time when God's laws were obeyed, the powerful were just and compassionate, life was orderly, and when "Every man could sit under his fig and vine and none would make him afraid". As such, the book of Ruth, while writing of the past, stimulates us to imagine a utopia that is not a dream. The subtle combination of art and morality makes Ruth a joy to read.

The Book of Ruth   1:1–6

I

In the days when heroes ruled **Israel and Judah**
A famine struck the Land. **So**
A certain man from Bethlehem, in **the land of Judah, decided**
To go and live in the Land of Moab.
He, his wife and two sons.
Elimelech[1]
was the name of the man
The name of his wife was Naomi[2].
The names of his two sons were
Mahlon[3] and
Chilion[4].
They were Ephratim[5]
Living in Bethlehem, **which was in the land of** Judah.
When they reached the Land of Moab,
They settled there.

Elimelech, Naomi's husband, died,
She and her two sons were bereft
They took as wives two women of Moab
The name of one was Orpah[6],
The name of the second was Ruth[7].
They lived there **for another** ten years. **Then**
Mahlon and Chilion also **were smitten and** died.
So the woman was bereft of **both** her sons and her husband.
In the Land of Moab she heard **rumours** that

[1] 'My God is King'.
[2] 'Pleasantness'.
[3] 'Disease'.
[4] 'Withering away'.
[5] The meaning is unclear, perhaps of aristocratic lineage.
[6] 'She turns away'.
[7] 'Friendship'.

The LORD had taken into account the plight of his people,
And decided to end the famine
And to give them bread.
So, she and her daughters-in-law made ready to go home.
As she and her daughters-in-law set out
To return to the Land of Judah,
She remonstrated with them:
"Each of you should go back to your mother's house.
Let the LORD deal kindly with you,
As you have dealt kindly with **my** dead **sons** and me.
God bless you
And let both of you find solace
In the home of a husband."
She kissed **and embraced** them.
Weeping aloud, they said, "No,
We will return with you to your people."
Naomi persisted. "Go back, my daughters.
Why do you want to come with me?
I have told you of the custom of the Israelites:
Had I other sons, you being childless,
They would have taken you
To give you sons
So that their dead brothers would have a
Name and inheritance in Israel.
But, have I any more sons in my womb
To become your husbands?
Turn back, my daughters, go!
You know I am too old to find a husband,
Even if I were to think, yes, there is hope for me,
Indeed **say that, a miracle,** I was possessed by a man last
    night,
Better yet even **conceived and** bore sons,
Would you wait until they grew up?
Would you remain chaste for them,
Holding yourselves apart from marrying other men?

Do not persist, my daughters, **believe me**
My embittered state is too great for you to share.
For The LORD's hand has assaulted me.

Again they wept,
And their tears became words
Expressing their wretchedness, their love and their sympathy
For each other.
But Orpah kissed her mother-in-law **good-bye**
And turned back to the road by which they had come.
But Ruth clung to her
Saying that she would not leave her.
Naomi spoke **imploringly and softly,**
"See, your sister-in-law has gone back to her kin
And to her gods.
You too should go.
Catch up with your sister-in-law."
Ruth pleaded: "Do not make me leave you
And stop me from following you.
For where you go will I go
And where you lie down will I lie down.
Your people are my people
And your God is my God.
In the place where you die, I will die,
And my burial place will be there.
Let The LORD take my life away,
And **punish** me even more
If anything but death separates us."
When she saw that **there was no dissuading her**
For she had made up her mind to go with her,
She **relented and** said no more.
The two travelled together until
They reached Bethlehem.
Their arrival in Bethlehem caused a commotion:
The women, **not believing their eyes,** cried out:

Could this be **the** Naomi **who left us?**
She answered them.
"No, I am no longer Naomi,
Call me Marah[1],
Because The LORD has made my life exceedingly bitter.
In fullness, I left you, but
The LORD has brought me back empty-handed **and desolate.**
How can you call me Naomi,
When **my wretchedness shows that** The LORD
Has found evidence against me,
Enough to afflict me with **so much** evil?"
So did Naomi,
With Ruth, the Moabite woman, her daughter-in-law,
Return from the Land of Moab.
Their arrival at Bethlehem was
At the beginning of the harvest of barley.

II
Before leaving for Moab with her family
Naomi knew a man of
The family of Elimelech, her husband.
A man with much property and integrity,
His name was Boaz[2].

Ruth, the Moabite woman, said to Naomi,
Allow me **as is the custom in this land** to
Go to the fields and
Pick up the ears of barley **that**
Accidentally fall from the hands of the reapers
Which is the poor folk's due.
I will find a reaper to follow
Who may be kind to me.

---

[1] 'Bitter one'.
[2] 'In him is strength'.

Naomi did not wish her to go,
To suffer the embarrassment of the poor
And to be scorned by the men in the fields.
But, seeing their hunger, Naomi consented:
"Go, my daughter. God bless you with good fortune."
So she arrived at the fields.
She was given permission
And she gleaned.
It so happened that the field belonged to Boaz,
Of the family of Elimelech, her father-in-law.
Work stopped as the hands saw that
Boaz had arrived from Bethlehem.
He greeted his reapers,
"The LORD be with you,"
And they greeted him,
"And may The LORD bless you."
Then Boaz seeing a beautiful woman in the field asked his
Servant, who was in charge of the harvesters,
"To whom does that woman belong?"
The overseer of the harvesters answered him:
"She is a girl from Moab
Who returned with Naomi
From the Land of Moab,
And she asked of us, ever so politely,
"Allow me to glean and pick up
from among the sheaves as
I follow the reapers."
This she has done from early morning until now.
Only now is she coming to the hut for a break.
Boaz walked over to her and said to Ruth:
"Pay attention, my daughter,
Do not glean in other men's fields.
In fact, do not leave this one.
Stay close to my hand girls . . .
See which part of the field they are reaping

And follow in their footsteps.
I have instructed my men not to harass you.
Also, if you are thirsty, go to the jugs
And drink of the water my boys have drawn."
She fell upon her face,
Touching the ground and said to him:
"What have I done that
You should be so kind to me,
To take any notice of me,
Seeing that I am nothing but a foreigner?"
Boaz answered her:
"I have often heard of all that
You have done for your mother-in-law,
After the death of your husband
How you left your father and mother,
And the land of your birth
To come to a people who were strange to you.
May The Lord reward your good work
May your compensation from The Lord, the God of Israel,
Under whose **sheltering** wings you have come
To find protection, be full."

She said: "You, my lord, have been very kind to me,
You have comforted me,
Your words have warmed the heart of your maidservant,
Even though I am not one of them."
At mealtime, Boaz beckoned to her,
"Come, share in the food.
Dip your portion in vinegar."
She sat by the side of the reapers.
He offered her roasted grain.
She ate her fill and had some left over
Which she put into her apron.
When she got up to glean some more
Boaz ordered his men with these words:

"Let her glean **freely** among the sheaves,
Do not embarrass her **with any interference.**
Also, let some stalks fall from your bundles.
Leave them for her to pick up, and
Make no insulting remarks to her."
She gleaned until evening
Then she beat out the grain from
What she had gleaned
Which amounted to an ephah of barley.
She carried it into town.
Her mother-in-law saw the **large** amount she had gleaned.
Ruth took out the food she had not eaten
And gave it to her mother-in-law.
She **ate the food and** enquired of her:
"Where did you glean today?
Where did you achieve this?
Blessed be he who showed you such consideration."
She told her mother-in-law
In whose field she had worked.
When she said, "The name of the man
Who dealt with me today was Boaz,"
Naomi rejoiced with her daughter-in-law:
"Blessed be he, **Boaz**, to The LORD
Who has not forgotten to be kind
Both to the living and to the dead."
For Naomi told her **with great excitement**,
"That man is a relation.
One of our redeemers:
He is among those duty-bound
To beget a son for a relative's childless widow,
To give the dead a remembrance and a place
Among the households of Israel."

Ruth, **equally excited**, told her,
"He was exceedingly generous.

He insisted that I remain close
To his workers until the end of the harvest."
Naomi told Ruth, her daughter-in-law,
"It is best for you, my daughter,
To go out only with his women **reapers**
And as not to be molested in any other field."
She kept close to the maidens of Boaz
And she gleaned to the end of both
The barley and wheat harvests.
All this time, she lived with her mother-in-law
And supported her.

III

And Naomi, her mother-in-law, said to her:
"As you have behaved like my daughter,
Should I not seek your security and welfare?
Now listen: Is Boaz not family?
The man with whose maidens you were **gleaning?**
Tonight he will be winnowing barley on the threshing floor.
So bathe yourself and put on perfume and your **finest** dress
And go down to the threshing floor.
But do not let anyone see you,
Until he has finished eating and drinking.
When he goes to sleep
And you see the place where he is lying down,
You will go there, uncover his legs
And lie down **next to him**
And he will tell you what to do."

Ruth said to Naomi, her mother-in-law:
"Is this not a wanton thing to do?
He is an older man and will think of me as a harlot
When I lie down next to him.
Should you not speak to him and ask him
To take me as his wife for the sake of your dead son?"

Naomi said:
"No, my daughter, in the light of the sober sun,
He will not wish to accept the responsibility.
For he has other family responsibilities,
And will not wish to give of his legacy
To your son conceived in Mahlon's name.
But in the night of his thanksgiving
For a rich harvest of wheat and barley,
And when he has eaten and drunk well,
And sees your lovely face by his side,
He may be generous
And wish to fulfil The Lord's commandment,
To raise a son for his dead kinsman.
Listen to me, my daughter,
And let us put our trust in God
Under whose wings you have taken shelter."

And she nodded in agreement and said to her:
"Tell me what to do and what to say
And I will do it."
So she bathed and massaged her body with oils.
Naomi brushed her hair a hundred times and then dressed her.
They rehearsed what Ruth was to do and to say.
When dusk began to fall,
Naomi walked with Ruth to the gates of Bethlehem.
She kissed her and said:
"May The Lord bless you as you go out
And bless you on your return."
The watchman closed the gates behind her
As she walked towards the fields.

Unseen she arrived at the threshing floor
and acted as her mother-in-law had advised.
She could see the men eating and drinking and laughing.
When Boaz had eaten and drunk as much as he could
He was feeling very happy.

45

He lay down by a heap of barley **and slept.**
Ruth approached quietly,
Uncovered his legs
And lay down **by him.**
In the middle of the night
The man was startled **by her touch.**
He turned and there was a woman by his legs.
He demanded: "And who are you?"
She answered, "I am Ruth, your maidservant.
Please, spread the wings of your cloak over your maidservant,
Because you have the right to redeem me
From my childlessness and widowhood."
He said, "May the LORD bless you, my daughter,
For the kindness you now show is
Greater than the kindnesses you have done until now.
For you could have pursued
Younger men, either rich or poor.

But instead you sought a redeemer to
Give your dead husband an
Eternal name and place among his brethren.
Now, my daughter, do not be afraid.
I will do what you ask,
And I will gladly do so.
For all the elders of my people,
Who sit **and give judgement** by the **town** gates,
Know that you are a woman of integrity.
But while it is true
I have the right of your redemption,
There is a kinsman even closer than myself.
Stay the night
And in the morning we will see:
If he will redeem you, so be it.
But if he does not choose to do this,
By the life of the LORD

I shall act as your redeemer.
Until then, lie here until the morning
So that you are not seen or disgraced."

She lay by him until the breaking of dawn.
She got up while it was still too dark
For people to recognize each other.
He said to his servants:
"Let no one know that a woman came to the threshing floor."
To her he said: "Bring me your cloak and hold it out."
She held it, and he gave her
Six measures of barley,
He made it comfortable for her to carry
And so she entered the town.

When she came to her mother-in-law, she asked:
"Who are you, my daughter?"
"Surely you recognize your Ruth?"
"Of course I do, but I wanted to know
Whether you were still only my daughter-in-law,
Or the woman engaged to Boaz?"
So she told her all that the man had done for her.
She said: "These six measures of barley he gave to me,
Saying, 'Do not go empty-handed to your mother-in-law.'
And she told her of his promise regarding her redemption.
Then she said: "Be patient, my daughter,
For soon we will know what will happen **to you**
For this man will not rest
Until the matter is settled,
and it will be done today!"

IV

Boaz went up to the *town* gate
And sat himself down **among the other leading citizens.**
Soon, the kinsman of whom Boaz spoke was passing by.

Boaz called, "You there, come here and sit down."
He turned around and sat down.
And he collected ten elders and told them to sit **by him**
And they sat.
He said to the kinsman:
"You know that piece of land,
Which belonged to our brother Elimelech,
Well, Naomi wishes to sell the right to redeem it,
For her husband had sold it
Before they left for Moab.
Now that she has returned from Moab,
And I thought it best to say to you
In the presence of the elders of the people
Who are sitting here:
If you wish **to buy it back into the family** buy it,
If you wish to exercise the right of redemption, do so.
But if you do not wish to do it,
Tell me so that I will know,
Because other than you
There is no one to redeem it,
excepting me, as I am the next in line."

He replied: "I will redeem it."
Boaz continued: **"You are aware** that on the day
You buy the **right of redeeming the** field from Naomi,
You buy it also from Ruth, the Moabite woman,
The wife of the dead, whom you must likewise redeem
To establish the name of the dead upon his inheritance.
By giving her a son."
The kinsman **changed his mind and** said:
"I cannot **exercise the duty of redemption**
For I would affect my legacy **to my own children.**
You do it as I am not able to."

Now this was the custom a long time ago in Israel
In matters of redemption and purchase:

The confirmation of all matters
Was for a man
To take off his shoe
And give it to his fellow
So the kinsman said to Boaz,
In the presence of witnesses,
"Buy it yourself."
And he took off his shoe.
So, Boaz said to the elders
And all who were there,
"You are witnesses today
That I have purchased
All that belongs to Elimelech
And all that was Chilion's and Mahlon's from Naomi.
In so doing, also Ruth the Moabite woman,
The wife of Mahlon, I do acquire as my wife
To establish the name of the dead
and to give him
Through the son Ruth will bear for me
His inheritance **in Israel.**
I do this so that the name of the dead man
Will not disappear among his brothers
And from the place where he lived.
Of this, you are **all** witnesses today."

All the people who were by the gate,
And all the elders said:
"We are witnesses **to what you have done.**
May the LORD bless the woman
Who enters your home.
May she be like Rachel and Leah, the wives of Jacob,
Who between them established the House of Israel.
Grow strong in Ephratah
Be renowned in Bethlehem
May your household become like that of Perez

Whom Tamar bore to Judah, **the son of Israel,**
By the children that the LORD will give you
Through this young woman."
Boaz took Ruth,
And she became his wife.
And he went in to her
And the LORD blessed her womb
And she bore a son.
The women congratulated Naomi,
"Praised be the LORD
Who this day has not left you without a descendant[1]
To perpetuate the family name,
Who will give you a new lease of life
And be a stay in your old age.
Truly, your daughter-in-law,
Who so loves you, has given birth to him,
She who has served you better than seven sons."
Naomi took the boy, clasping him to her bosom,
And served him as nurse.
The women neighbours gave him their own designation,
Saying: "There is a son born to Naomi."
He was called Obed[2].
He was the father of Jesse
Who was the father of David.

*　　　　　*　　　　　*

So this is the genealogy of David,
The great grandson of Ruth and Boaz.
Judah fathered Perez by his daughter-in-law Tamar
Perez was the father of
Hezron, of

---

[1] Literally a redeemer. i.e. to carry on the family line of her husband Elimelech
and son Mahlon.
[2] 'Servant'.

Ram, of
Amminadab, of
Nahshon, of
Salmon, of
Boaz, of
Obed, of
Jesse, of
David, **king of Judah and Israel**.

APPENDIX I

The Law of the Levirate Marriage
DEUTERONOMY 25:5–10

When brothers dwell together and one of them dies and leaves no son, the wife of the deceased shall not be married to a stranger, outside the family. Her husband's brother shall unite with her: he shall take her as his wife and perform the Levirate's duty. The first son that she bears shall be accounted to the dead brother, that his name may not be blotted out in Israel.   *Deut 25:5–7*

But if the man does not want to marry his brother's widow, his brother's widow shall appear before the elders in the gate and declare, "My husband's brother refuses to establish a name in Israel for his brother; he will not perform the duty of the Levir." The elders of the town shall then summon him and talk to him. If he insists, saying, "I do not want to marry her", his brother's widow shall go up to him in the presence of the elders, pull the sandal off his foot, spit in his face, and make this declaration: "This shall be done to the man who will not build up his brother's house! And he shall go in Israel by the name of the family of the one without a sandal."   *Deut 25:7–10*

APPENDIX II

The Tragic Consequences of the Law of the Levir
GENESIS 38   *Er and Onan, Judah and Tamar*

The importance and consequences of the law of the Levir are illustrated by a chapter of Genesis. The following tale reveals: 1) the emphasis placed on continuing the line of a deceased male who has left no heirs; 2) the punishment by God of individuals who transgressed against the intention of the law; 3) the continuation of the marital bond after the death of the husband. Tamar is condemned for adultery even though her husband is dead because she must wait for Judah's remaining son to give her a child; 4) the power of the Patriarch – in this instance Judah – to dispense justice and allow for ameliorating circumstances; 5) the power of the Patriarchs to ignore other precedents – Perez, the child of Tamar and Judah, the product of an incestuous relationship (father and daughter-in-law) should be considered a *Mamzer* and suffer the consequences. [See introduction about the Mamzer] Perez is not considered a Mamzer, and indeed, as the genealogy of David at the end of the story of Ruth indicates, was the ancestor of Boaz. It must be more than coincidence that the author of Ruth should insert the ceremony required for the Levir who rejects his responsibility when the only other biblical episode of a Levirate marriage refers to the ancestor of Boaz.

APPENDIX III

Did Ruth have twins?

There is some obscurity at the end of the story about the birth and naming of Ruth's child. Herbert Chanan Brichto [HUC Annual 1973, Cincinnati] speculates on the possibility that, in the original rendition, Ruth, like Boaz's great ancestress Tamar (Appendix II), gave birth to twins. He cites the fact that the elders of Bethlehem ask that Boaz be blessed with children from Ruth. If she had been blessed with twins, the first born would have, so to speak, preserved the continuity of Elimelech and Naomi's line through Mahlon, for whom Boaz acted as 'the redeemer', and the second would have, so to speak, belonged to Boaz alone. The other blessing asked by the Elders for Boaz was that Ruth be like both Rachel and Leah, the wives of Jacob who between them established the House of Israel. This also suggests that Ruth should have two children, one to establish the family continuity of Mahlon, his dead kinsman; this was the child of whom the neighbours said: "There is a son born to Naomi." The other twin would have to establish the line of Boaz. This was the child who according to the story was named Obed.

The emphasis on the obligation of the Levirate marriage high-lights the great importance given in the Bible to preserving the continuity of a family line, from whom there were no children, and also the dependance of the dead on the living to give them respect so that they might enjoy peace in the after-life.

Lamentations

Lamentations

Traditionally, Lamentations was written by the prophet Jeremiah. For this reason it follows the works of that prophet in the Christian order of the Hebrew Bible. A careful reading of the Five Chapters which I have designated as three laments, the Laments of the Suffering Servant and a Prayer for Salvation would indicate more than one author, if only because certain chapters reveal greater genius than others.

It is of interest to note that, in the original Hebrew, Lament 1 and 2 (Chapters 1 and 2) each has 22 verses reflecting the number of letters in the Hebrew alphabet and that the first verse begins with the first letter of the alphabet [*Aleph*] and progresses through the alphabet until the last letter [*Tawf*]. The Lament of the Suffering Servant (Chapter 3) has 66 verses, the first three verses each beginning with *Aleph* and so on with three verses beginning with succeeding letters of the Hebrew alphabet. Lament 4 (Chapter 4) follows the pattern of Lament 1 and 2 with the same alphabetical acrostic. The Prayer for Salvation (Chapter 5) also has 22 verses but with no alphabetical ordering.

This tight but varying structure suggests both that its purpose was to make it easier to memorize for use at public occasions and that certain chapters may have been added later. Lamentations must have been composed sometime between the end of the sixth century BCE, when Judea was conquered by the Babylonians, and the third century BC.

Its heartrending cries are chanted in synagogues to commemorate the destruction of the Temple on the ninth day of the Jewish month of Ab (sometime in August) at the end of a twenty-four-hour fast beginning at nightfall. So striking are the laments that, as I began the task of translation, I heard the first few verses involuntarily ringing in my ears in the traditional cantillation. As a dirge for the destruction of a once-proud nation reduced to servitude and humiliation, I do not believe it can be equalled.

Lamentations

THE FIRST LAMENT

How desolate sits the city
Once crowded with people
How like a widow she has become
Once mighty among the nations
Once the princess of the provinces
She is now a vassal state.

Sobbing ceaselessly throughout the night,
Her tears running down her cheeks
Not for her a comforter
From all her former lovers
All her friends betrayed her
They have become her enemies.

Judah has gone into exile
Driven by oppression and harsh labour
She lives now among the Gentiles
She finds no contentment.
All her pursuers caught up with her
Between the straits of despair.

The roads to Zion are in mourning –
No pilgrims to attend her festivals
All her gates are in ruins
Her priests groan
Her young girls are terror-stricken
Bitterness is Zion's fate.

Her opponents have taken charge
Her enemies relax in luxury
For the Lord has punished her

For her numerous wrong doings
Her very infants have gone into captivity
In front of the enemy.

Vanished from the Daughter of Zion
Is all her splendour
Her princes are like stags
Who find no place to pasture
They flee with no strength
Before their hunters.

Jerusalem can but remember
In the time of her oppression and wandering
All the lovely things she once had.
Before her people fell into the hands of the enemy
When there was no one to help her
Her opponents looked upon her and laughed at her destruction.

Jerusalem has surely done wrong
Therefore she has become an outcast
All who respected her now humiliate her
Because they have seen her nakedness
She can only moan **in self-pity**
And turn her face away **in shame.**

Her filth clings to her skirts
She never considered the consequences of her behaviour
Her downfall was spectacular
She has no comforter.
"See O Lord how great is my misery
For the enemy has prevailed."

The enemy has stretched out his hand
Over all that she held most precious
She looked at the Gentiles
As they entered her Temple.

Those whom you commanded
Never to enter into your congregation.

All the people are moaning
They are looking for bread
They exchange their jewellery for food
To bring them back to life.
"See O LORD and look carefully
How abject I have become."

May it never happen to you
All you who pass this way
Look and see if there is any pain equal to my pain
With which I have been afflicted
With which the LORD has struck me
On the day of his anger.

It is as if from high
He sent fire into my bones
He spread a net to ensnare my feet
He has made me turn back
He has left me shattered
I am dizzy the whole day.

The burden of my sins is tightly bound
He strings them all together
They are placed on my neck
He saps my strength
The LORD has given me into the hands
Of those against whom I cannot stand.

The LORD has made me as nothing
And all the warriors within my ranks
He has appointed against me a solemn assembly
To crush my young men
As in a wine press the LORD has trodden
The virgin daughters of Judah.

For all these things I do weep
My eyes stream down with tears
Because far from me is any comforter
Someone to revive my spirit
My children are desolate
Because the enemy is triumphant.

Zion spreads out her hands in prayer
There is none to give her comfort
The LORD has given a command in regard to Jacob
That all around her should oppose her
Jerusalem has become an outcast
Amongst them.

Righteous is the LORD
For I have rebelled against his command
Please listen all you nations
Behold my agony
My young girls and young men
Have gone into captivity.

I cried out for my lovers
They have deceived me
My priests and my elders
Perished in the city
They were looking for food
To keep themselves alive

See O LORD how distressed I am
My bowels are churning
My heart turns upside down within me
Because I have been very rebellious
Outside the sword causes bereavement
Inside is the stillness of death.

They have heard that I am groaning
There is still none to comfort me

All my enemies have heard of my disaster and are glad
But this is your doing
You will bring the day of your reckoning
And they will be as I am

Let all their wrong doings come before you
Do to them
What you have done to me
For all my sins
For my groaning is unending
And my heart is faint.

*   *   *

THE SECOND LAMENT

How the LORD covered with a dark cloud
The daughter of Zion in his anger **with her**
He has hurled down from the heavens to the ground
The glory that was once Israel
He did not even remember his footstool[1]
On the day of his anger

The LORD has swallowed up without mercy
All the pasture lands of Jacob
In his anger he has overthrown
The fortress cities of the daughters of Judah
He has thrown them to the ground
He has humiliated his kingdom and its princes.

In unrelenting rage
He has destroyed all of Israel's defences
He has pulled back his right hand **of power**
From before the enemy.
Instead he has caused Jacob to burn like a fire in flame

---

[1] The sanctuary – the Holy of Holies – in The Temple. The image is of God enthroned in heaven with his feet resting on his footstool on earth.

Which consumes everything around it.

As an enemy, he has bent his bow
He stands using his mighty right hand as an opponent would
He wipes out all that gave delight
In the dwellings of the daughters of Zion
He releases his fury like fire.

The LORD has become like an enemy
He has swallowed up Israel
He has swallowed all her citadels
He has demolished her fortresses
For the daughter of Judah he has been
The cause of unceasing moaning and groaning.

He has stripped clean his Temple as one does a garden shed
He has destroyed the meeting points for worship
The LORD has made Zion forget
Festivals and the Sabbath
In the ferocity of his rage
He has rejected both king and priest.

The LORD has despised his altar
He has hated his holy sanctuary
He has handed over to the enemy
The walls of her citadels
Their shouts of triumph in the House of the LORD are
As it was on days of festive celebrations.

The LORD has decided to destroy
The protecting walls of the daughter of Zion
He has drawn the line of destruction
He will not hold back his hand from destruction
He has made wall and rampart to mourn
Together they fall into ruins.

Her gates are battered into the ground
He has demolished and destroyed their cross-bars

Kings and princes are exiles among the nations
There is no Torah
Even her prophets receive
No vision from the LORD.

They sat upon the ground stunned into silence:
These are the elders of the daughters of Zion
They heap dust over their heads
They clothe themselves in sackcloth
They bow their heads to the ground:
These are the young girls of Jerusalem.

My eyes cannot make any more tears
My bowels are turning over within me
My feelings pour over the ground
Because of the ruination of the daughters of my people
Babes and sucklings faint away
In the city squares.

They cry out for their mothers,
"Where is there food and drink?"
They faint as do wounded soldiers
On the city's squares
As they let go of their lives
Clinging to their mothers' breasts.

How shall I bear witness to your destruction
To what could I compare you, O daughter of Jerusalem
If I could compare your plight to others
I could console you, O daughter of Zion
But your destruction is as vast as the sea
Who is there to heal you?

What your seers prophesied for you
Had no substance but was illusory
They did not reveal the depth of your sinfulness
To enable you to prevent your captivity

But they gave you visions
Laden with delusions and deceptions.

All passers-by clap their hands at you
They hiss and shake their heads
At **the misfortune of** the daughter of Jerusalem:
Is this then the city that they called
The perfection of beauty
The joy of the whole world?

All your enemies open up wide their mouths against you.
They hiss and gnash their teeth **with satisfaction.**
They say, "We have swallowed her up
This is the day we were hoping for
It has come for us
We have seen it **at last.**"

No, it was the LORD who executed his plan
He has fulfilled his warning **of punishment**
When he commanded us in ancient days
He has torn down without pity
He has allowed the enemy to rejoice over you
He has increased the forces of your enemy.

Their hearts cry out to the LORD
The very walls of the daughter of Zion
Let your tears run down like a river
Day and night
Give yourself no rest
Give your eyes **no end to crying.**

Up, cry out in the night
At the change of every night watch
Pour out your heart like water in the presence of the LORD
Lift up your hands towards him **in prayer**
For the lives of your youngsters that faint from hunger
At the corner of every street.

See O Lord look closely
Against whom have you done this
Did you intend mothers to eat the fruits of their womb
The very infants they fondled?
Did you intend that priest and prophet
Should be slaughtered in the Lord's Temple?

The young and old lie down in the streets
Young women and men fall by the sword
You have slain them in the day of your anger
You have slaughtered
You have shown no mercy.

You have summoned as on a festival
My enemies to terrify me from all sides
On the day of the Lord's anger
There were no refugees nor survivors
Even those children I fondled and raised
My enemy has swallowed them up.

*   *   *

THE LAMENT OF THE SUFFERING SERVANT

I am the person who understood affliction under the rod of his
    anger
Guiding me, he made me walk not in light but in darkness
Only against me does he turn his might day and night.

He has wasted away my flesh and skin and broken my bones
He built a wall around me of bitterness and misery
He makes me live in dark places as those long dead.

He has fenced me in so that I cannot escape – the fetters are
    heavy.
Even when I cry calling for help he shuts our my prayers
He has blocked my ways with stones and has obstructed my
    paths.

He is for me like a bear lying in wait, like a lion in ambush
He has led me in the wrong direction, torn me to shreds and
    destroyed me
He has bent his bow making me the target for his arrows.

He has pierced deep inside me with the arrows of his quiver
I became a laughing stock for all the nations – their taunts day
    and night
With bitterness, he has satisfied me; he has sated me with
    wormwood.

He has chipped my teeth with sand; He has pressed my face in
    the dust.
My life is so bereft of any peace, that I cannot remember the
    good times
I said, "I have lost my strength; also any hope in the Lord.

The memory of my affliction and my anguish is wormwood
    and gall
I cannot stop thinking of it and my spirit sinks within me
This is what I must bring back to mind to give me hope:

The mercy of the Lord is not spent, His compassion not ended
They arise afresh in the morning; great is your faithfulness:
"The Lord is my portion," I say. "Therefore I will hope in
    him."

The Lord is good to those who wait for him, to those who seek
    him.
It is best for one to wait in silence for the Lord's salvation
It is best for a person to accept discipline during his youth.

Let the unfortunate sit alone and be silent because this is what
    he laid upon him
Let him put his face to the ground; maybe there is still hope
Let him turn his cheek to those who strike him; let him enjoy
    reproach.

But the LORD will not cast off forever
Though he brings grief he will have pity because of the
　greatness of his love.
He does not want to cause affliction or grief for the sons of
　men:

To crush underfoot all the prisoners of earth
To turn aside the rights that a man has before the Most High
To betray a man in his righteous cause – of this the LORD does
　not approve.

Who can say that something happened without the LORD
　discerning it?
Does not evil as well as good emanate from the Most High?
Why do living mortals complain – especially men who have
　sinned?

Let us search and examine our ways and return to the LORD
Let us put our hearts in our hands and lift them up to God in
　heaven
We have sinned and rebelled – You have not pardoned.

You have enveloped us in rage and pursued us, killing without
　mercy
You have hidden yourself behind a cloud so that no prayer
　may pass.
You have made us as rubbish and refuse among the nations.

All our enemies have opened their mouths wide against us
Terror and trembling have come upon us – desolation and
　destruction.
My eyes pour out rivers of tears over the destruction of my
　people.

My eyes will not stop gushing with tears
Until the LORD looks down and sees from heaven
How my eyes have become sore over **grieving** for the daughters
　of my city.

Like an innocent bird my enemies have chased me for no
    reason
Casting me in a pit they cut off my life and heap stones upon
    me
My head is overcome with water; I thought, "I am finished."

I called out your name, O LORD from the deepest pit
You have heard my voice; do not close your ears to my cry for
    relief
You used to draw near when I called you; you said, "Do not be
    afraid."

You used to defend me, you would save my life
O LORD you have seen how I have been wronged; judge me
    favourably.
You have witnessed their vengeance, all their plots against me.

You have heard their taunts, O LORD, and all their plans
    against me
The whispering and murmuring of my enemies day and night.
See how when they sit or stand I have become their song of
    derision.

Punish them O LORD as the deeds of their hands deserve
Give them hardness of heart so that you may curse them **even
more.**
Pursue them in anger and destroy them from under the
    heavens of the LORD.

             *   *   *

THE FOURTH LAMENT

How has the gold become tarnished
How has the pure gold altered itself
The sacred stones lie scattered
At every street corner.

The dear sons of Zion
Comparable to noble gold
How now are they despised as earthenware
The work of a potter's hands.

Even jackals draw out their breast
They give suck to their cubs
But the daughters of my people have become cruel
Like ostriches in the wilderness.[1]

The tongue of the suckling child
Sticks to its mouth in **dryness of** thirst
They beg for bread
There is no one to break a crust for them.

They who used to feed on delicacies
Lie destitute in the streets
They that were raised in scarlet
Grasp piles of rubbish in search of food.

Why, for the sins of the daughter of my people
Are more than the sins of Sodom
That was overwhelmed in an instant
Without a human hand touching her.

Her princes were as fine as snow
They were whiter than milk
Their bodies were rosier than coral
They shone like sapphire.

Now their faces are blacker than soot
They are not recognizable in the streets
Their skin is shrivelled over their bones
As dry as dead wood.

Those slain by the sword are better off

[1] Ostriches had the reputation of putting themselves before their young when food was scarce. Destitution has deprived Israel of its natural instincts.

Than those who perish from famine
Wasting away, pierced through **by hunger**
For the need of the produce of the field.

The hands of compassionate women
Have cooked their own children[1]
They became food for them
So great has been the destruction of the daughters of my
    people.

The LORD's anger has been fully vented
He has poured out his fierce rage
He has kindled a fire in Zion
Which has consumed her very foundations.

The kings of the earth could not believe
Nor could the inhabitants of the world
That the foe and enemy could storm
The gates of Jerusalem.

It is because of the sins of her prophets
And the iniquities of her priests
Who in their midst have
Shed the blood of the righteous.

They stumble like blind men in the streets
They are defiled with **innocent** blood[2]
So that men are unable
To touch their clothes.

"Go away, unclean men," people call out to them.

---

[1] Jeremiah hyperbolically prophesies the outcome of God's punishment
(Jeremiah 19:19). Did it happen? Or is this description based on Jeremiah's
prophecy? Could mothers really turn their children into food?
[2] Ancient Israel, as well as other cultures, had the concept of ritual
uncleanness requiring physical ablutions such as baptism. The guilty priests
and prophets have become unclean through their moral perversions. In ancient
cultures pollution is contagious.

"Go away, do not touch anything."
So they fled and wandered off. So it was said among the
    nations,
"No longer shall they live here."

The Presence of the LORD used to be their portion
Now, he will take no notice of them.
They did not respect the priests of righteousness
Nor did they show favour to the elders.

Our eyes still become bleary
Waiting in vain for our help
We keep watching and waiting
For an ally nation that could save us.

They are behind every one of our steps
They prevent us from congregating in the squares
Our end is approaching. All our days are spent
For our end has come.

Swifter were those who pursued us
Than the eagles of heaven.
They chased us on the mountain tops
They lay in ambush for us in the wilderness.

The very breath of our existence, the LORD's Anointed [the
    king],
Was cast into their dungeons
Of whom, we had said, "Under his protection
We shall survive among the peoples."

Rejoice and be glad O daughters of Edom
You who live in the land of Uz
Soon the **bitter** cup will be passed on to you
You shall become drunk and reveal your nakedness.

The punishment for your iniquity is complete, O Daughters of
    Zion

No more will you be carried off into captivity.
Now, he will punish your iniquity, O Daughters of Edom
Your sins will be revealed.

*   *   *

A PRAYER FOR REDEMPTION

Consider O LORD what has befallen us
Look closely and see the extent of our disgrace!

Our inheritance is turned over to strangers
Our homes to aliens.

We have become orphans without a father
Our mothers are **defenceless as** widows.

We had to pay to drink our own water
Our kindling wood is obtainable only at a price.

We are pursued up to our necks
We are exhausted and find no rest.

We have submitted ourselves to Egypt
And to Syria to get enough bread.

Our fathers who sinned are no longer **with us**
And we have suffered because of their sins.

Servants rule over us
With none to rescue us from them.

We get our food by putting our lives in peril
Because of the **marauders'** swords in the waste places.

Our skin is as hot as an oven
Because of the fever of famine.

They have raped the women in Zion
The virgins in the cities of Judah.

Princes are hung up by their hands
The presence of the elders is treated with no respect.

Young men carry millstones
And children stumble under the wood **they carry.**

No more do elders sit by the gate
The lads no longer play their music.

The joy in our heart has gone
Our dance has turned into mourning.

The crown is fallen from our head
Woe unto us because we have sinned

For this our heart is weary
Because of these things our eyes become blank.

And Mount Zion which lies desolate.
The foxes walk over it.

You O LORD live in eternity
Your throne is from generation to generation.

Why will you forget us forever
And forsake us for all time?

Turn us unto you O LORD and we will return
Renew our days as of old
Unless you have entirely rejected us
And are angry with us beyond any limits.

Ecclesiastes

Introduction

Koheleth, known also as Ecclesiastes, most assuredly was not the wise King Solomon, nor was he any king. The advice he gives to cope with the volatility or displeasure of monarchs might indicate that he was a courtier subject to the mood swings of his ruler. His claim that as king he had known it all, seen it all and had achieved more wealth than any royal predecessor was to prove that wisdom, experience or riches are not the key to happiness.

The book was written after the return from exile and most likely during the turbulent period (circa second century) when the descendants of the Maccabees had achieved some level of independence from their neighbours and assumed the title of king. There have been suggestions that Koheleth had come under the influence of Hellenistic thought, hence his pessimistic philosophy of life. The inconsistency of his thoughts suggest, however, that in this work he is not attempting to present a coherent philosophy of life, but rather observations based on his experience over a lifetime.

The lack of purpose for human existence which seems to be the foundation of his pessimism seems to contradict the belief in a Creator which intervenes in the text. This could have been a pious insertion to justify including a most popular but heretical book in the Bible, or it could be the expression of faith of a man steeped in traditional Judaism whose experience often leads him to take a more cynical view.

The reader should appreciate the difficulties of translating this book. Often the morals are very cryptic – so much so that I have found different translations coming up with opposite meanings for the same text. In some instances, my translation had to be a paraphrase based on deductive reasoning and intelligent guesswork.

In a manner following the conclusion of Koheleth, I would say,

To sum it up,
All being considered,
Koheleth was a very wise man
He fulfilled his aim
'To create pleasing sayings
Well written and full of truth'.

Ecclesiastes 1:1–9

The words of Koheleth, son of David, king in Jerusalem!

Vanity of vanities, says Koheleth,[1]
Sheer futility, all is futile!
What profit has a person for all his labour,
Working under **the heat of** the sun.

Generations come and go
But the earth remains **the same** forever.
The sun rises, the sun sets and rushes
Back to the place from which it will arise **again.**

Blowing to the south
Then turning to the north,
The wind turns around and around
To its rounds does the wind return.

All streams flow into the sea,
But the sea does not overflow
To the source of the rivers,
They return to start flowing again.
All **such** thoughts are wearisome
No individual is able to articulate **the futility!**
Still, the eye can never see enough
Nor can the ear hear enough.
What was is what will be
What has been done is what will be done.
There is nothing new under the sun.

---

[1] It was customary for aspiring authors to attribute their writings to great men. The Hebrew Koheleth is derived from *kahal*, meaning community. It has thus been translated as Preacher. "Ecclesiastes" is the Greek equivalent.

Can there be a thing of which one can say,
See this is something new?
No, it has already been in worlds past
Which came before our own existence.

There is no memory of the early generations
Nor will there be any memory of
The later generations to come
By those who come after **them.**

I, Koheleth, king over Israel in Jerusalem,
Set my mind intelligently to investigate and explore
Everything achieved under the heavens.
It is an exercise in frustration
That God has given to human beings
With which to torture themselves.

I have observed all the labours performed under the sun;
And see – it is all futile; a chasing after the wind:
The crooked cannot be made straight.
What is missing cannot be counted.

When I rolled it over in my mind, I thought:
Look, I have become greater and wiser
Than all those who ruled over Jerusalem before me
And my mind had acquired much wisdom and knowledge.

I set my mind to learn wisdom
Also to experience foolishness and frivolity.
I realized that this too was chasing after the wind
For in much wisdom is much frustration
And to increase knowledge is to increase pain.

*　　　　*　　　　*

I thought to myself,
I will indulge myself with fun
And taste the good **life**

That also proved futile
To laugh is madness
And pleasure – where does it lead to?

I decided to drown my flesh with wine,
But to keep my wits about me:
To embrace joyous madness to learn
What is the best way for humans to behave
Under the heavens during the few days of their lives.

I increased my enterprises.
I built for myself stately homes
I planted for my pleasure vineyards
I made myself gardens and orchards.
I planted in them every kind of fruit tree
I made springs with enough water
To irrigate a forest covered with trees.

I bought slaves and maidens
In addition to the slaves born in my palace.

I had much cattle, herds and flocks
More than anyone owned in Jerusalem before me.

I also amassed silver and gold
Kings' treasures levied from the provinces.

I gathered men and women singers
All the delights of the flesh
And countless concubines.

So I increased and amassed more
Than all who came before me in Jerusalem
But kept my wits about me
And was not overwhelmed by what I had done.

But whatever my eyes lusted after
I did not deny them
I did not withhold myself from any pleasure

Because I rejoiced in all I had achieved.
This was my reward for all my efforts.

But then I looked at the works of my hands
And at the results of the efforts I had made –
My conclusion: All was in vain,
A chasing after the wind.
There was no value **in our lives** under the sun.

Next, I turned to consider wisdom
And **its opposites**, foolishness and frivolity.
For what can a person who follows the king
Do more than what has already been done.
I concluded: Wisdom is better than foolishness
As light is better than darkness.
The wise person has eyes in his head **to see**,
But the fool walks in darkness.

Still, I knew that one fate awaits them all.
In the depths of my heart, I realized:
The fate of the fool will be my fate.
What point, therefore, in my becoming so wise.
Even this thought, I said to myself, was pointless.

For there is no lasting memory
Of the wise or the fool
Because in the days to come
All will be forgotten
How can the wise die differently than the fools?

So I hated life
For all that was done under the sun
Was despicable to me
Because it was all in vain
And a chasing after the wind.

And I hated all that I had achieved under the sun
Because I would leave it to the man coming after me.

Who knows whether he will be wise or a fool?
Regardless, he will be the master of the fruits of my labour,
Achieved by my hard work and wisdom under the sun.
Even these thoughts are vain!

So I decided to indulge myself in despair
Over all that I had achieved under the sun,
How unfair that a person whose achievements
Were based on wisdom, experience and skill
Should give it as the legacy to the person
Who made no contribution to it.
Even the thought of this great injustice is in vain!

What is the reality for a person
Of all the work and planning
That he performs under the sun
For all his days are painful
His business causes stress.
Even at night, he cannot relax
The thought of this is also in vain!

There is no right course for a person
But to eat and drink
And give himself pleasure
From the profit of his labour.
Only this, I concluded, is the will of God.

For who will eat,
Who will enjoy
Except for his munificence?
To the person who pleases him,
He gives wisdom, knowledge and joy.

To the sinner, he gives the business
Of accumulating and piling up
To leave for him who pleases God.

Even this conclusion is in vain
And a chasing after the wind.

*   *   *

For everything its season
And a time for all human business
Under the heavens.

A time for giving birth and a time for dying
A time for planting and a time for plucking what has been
    planted.

A time for killing and a time for healing
A time for tearing down and a time for building.

A time for weeping and a time for laughing
A time for mourning and a time for dancing.

A time for throwing stones and a time for gathering stones
A time for embracing and a time to refrain from embracing.

A time for searching and a time for losing
A time for keeping and a time for discarding.

A time for tearing and a time for sewing
A time for silence and a time for talking.

A time for loving and a time for hating
A time for war and a time for peace.

What profit has the achiever from his work?
I have seen the business that God has given to mortals
With which to be occupied.
He has made everything appropriate to its time.
But also, he has put a sense of eternity in his heart
Without a person finding the meaning
Of what God has done from the beginning to the end.

I have decided that there is no right course for them,
But to be happy and achieve contentment in their lives.
And also, every man should eat and drink,
Seeing benefits for all his work –
It is the gift of God.

I understand that whatever God does
It will be for eternity.
Nothing can be added to it
And from it nothing can be subtracted.
The supreme God has done this
So that men may be in fear before him.

What is now has already been
What will be has already been
And God brings back again that which has disappeared.
Again, I have observed under the sun
In the courts of justice there was corruption.
In the councils where one expected the righteous,
There were criminals.

I thought: God will judge the righteous and the wicked
For there is a time for **judging** every human business
And for every act performed there **by men**.
I decided that, in regard to human beings,
They are not like the immortals but to realise
That they are no different than beasts.

The fate of humanity and the fate of the beast is the same.
As one dies, so the other dies.
They all have the same breath of life.
And the distinction of man over beast is nil.
And all is vanity.

All creatures are destined for the same place
All came out of the dust and
All will return to the dust.

Who knows that the human spirits fly upwards
And the animal spirit goes down into the earth?

So I understood that there is no better course
Than for a person to rejoice in his achievements
Since that is his only portion.
Who is there to let him know what will be after him?

*   *   *

I turned to consider all the acts of oppression
Committed under the sun.
Look at the tears of the oppressed.
They have no comforter
Their oppressors are backed by power
But they have no comforters.

So I praised the dead because they had died
More than the living who were still alive.
But better than both is he who is not yet born
Who has not seen the wicked work
That is done under the sun.

Also, I see that all effort and skilful art
Is the consequence of envy between men.
This thought also is in vain
And a chasing after the wind.

Still, the fool folds his hands together, **doing nothing**
And consumes his own flesh **through starvation.**
But **on the other hand**, better is a handful of contentment
Than both hands always busy and chasing after the wind.

Then I turned to consider the futility under the sun
There is one person without a companion
He has neither son nor brother **with whom to share**
Yet there is no end to his work.
Nor are his eyes ever satisfied by his wealth:

Well could he say, "For whom do I work,
Depriving myself of the pleasure **of recreation**.
This also is futile. It is a bad business."

Two are better than one
Because they prosper more from their shared labour.
For if they fall, one lifts up his friend.
But it is sad for one to fall,
Without a companion to raise him up.

When two lie together they keep each other warm
But how shall one person keep himself warm
While one can be overpowered by a robber
Two could defend themselves.
And a three-stranded rope is not easily torn.

It is better to be a poor but wise youth
Than an old but foolish king
Too arrogant to take advice
For out of the dungeon he came out to rule
Though the other born to become king became a pauper.

I considered all those that walked under the sun
Rallying in support of the youth who succeeded the king.
There was no counting all those he led
But those who came after will not praise him.
But these thoughts are also in vain
And a chasing after the wind.

Do not rush to the house of God
Rather go near to listen **to His commands**
This is preferable to the sacrifices of fools
Who only know how to do wrong.

*   *   *

Do not speak rashly
Nor be quick to speak before God

Because God is in the heavens
And you are **a mere mortal** on earth
Therefore, let your words be few.

For as dreaming comes from the pressures of business
So a fool's voice is heard when there are too many words.
When you make a vow to God, be quick to fulfil it.
For he has no desire for fools **who make promises without
      thinking.**
Whatever you vow, honour it.
Far better not to vow than to make a vow
Without honouring it.

So do not let your mouth bring guilt upon you[1]
And do not say to the messenger that it was a mistake.
Why would you incur God's anger by what you have said
And cause him to destroy what your hands have achieved?
Dreams of business success and trivia produce much talk.
Better that you fear God.

If you witness the oppression of the poor
The corruption of justice and the suppression of truth
In the councils of State do not be surprised.
For one higher official is preying upon another
And above both is another **taking his cut of the bribes**
The profit of the land is in their hands.
Even the wilderness is exploited by them when it is cultivated.[2]

A lover of money will never have enough money
And the lover of riches accrues no benefit from them,
But this too is a vain thought.

The more goods the more people to consume them.
What benefit does the owner have from them

---

[1] This seems to be an allusion to the promise to make an offering to the
Temple. The messenger is the Temple official who comes to collect the debt.
[2] The Hebrew of the last two lines is so obscure that the translation is primarily
a speculative grasp at the intention of the author based on the preceding lines.

Except to take pride in looking upon them?

Sweet is the sleep of a labourer,
Whether he had a lot or little to eat **before he slept**.
The wealth of the rich, however, does not allow them to sleep.

There is a tragic situation I have seen under the sun,
A man keeps close guard on his wealth and suffers for it.
For what if he loses wealth in a failed venture,
And has a son, and there is nothing to give him.
As he left his mother's womb,
So he will return naked just as he came.
He has nothing in his hand for all his labour.

Is this not a tragic business?
He must depart just as he came.
What benefit did he have for working for the wind?
All his days he eats in the gloom of darkness.
Full of anxiety depression and anger.

This is my conclusion of what is good:
It is pleasant to eat and drink,
To enjoy one's work under the sun
The full number of the days of his life
Given to him by God –
For this is his gift.

Every person to whom God has given wealth and possessions
And has given him the means to enjoy them;
To take what is allotted to him and to enjoy his work –
This is the gift of God.

Let him remember that the days of his life –
They are not many
And that God gives him work
For his own happiness.

*   *   *

There is an evil which I have experienced under the sun
It is very distressing for human kind.
God gives a person wealth, possessions and honour.
There is nothing that he lacks – no unfulfilled desire.
But then God does not give him the means to enjoy them
And a stranger enjoys their benefit
It is all so futile and tragic.

Even if a man had a hundred children
So that the years of his life are many;
But if he cannot enjoy the good things,
Even if he were never to die,
I say, the stillborn is better off.

Its[1] coming into the world was without purpose
Its departure is **dark with no meaning**.
Without a name its existence is obliterated.
It did not see the light of the sun
It had no experience **of life**
Still if he had lived two thousand years without pleasure
What difference would it have made
In the end, do we not all go to the same place?

All human labour is for his consumption, yet
The appetites are never satisfied.
What advantage does the wise have over the fool
Or the man of the world over the pauper?

It is better to enjoy what is before you
Than to pursue the object of desire.
But this thought is also vain
And a chasing after the wind.

Whoever comes into being,
His fate is already determined.

[1] The stillborn.

It is inescapable that he is a mere human
He cannot contend with that which is mightier than he – death.

Much philosophy with words
On the human condition
Increases the sense of futility.
What benefit does it give us?

For can anyone know
What is the best way for a human to live
During all his futile years
When he struts about like a shadow
No one can tell a person
What will come after him under the sun.

*   *   *

A good reputation is better than a sweet-smelling oil
And the day of death than the day of birth.
It makes better sense to go to the house in mourning
Than to the house full of festivities.
For that is the destiny of all humans.
Let the living keep this in their hearts.
The anxious contemplation **of death**
Is better than **hollow** laughter.

And a sad reflective face
May hide an enlightened mind.
Wise men find understanding in the houses of mourning
The minds of fools are dulled by those parties.
Better to hear the criticism of the wise
Than to listen to the songs of fools.
For as the rattling of empty barrels[1]
Is the laughter of fools.

---

[1] The Hebrew is 'The noise of thorns under a pot' which is cooking. The point is that a fool's laughter has no more significance than the crackling caused by the fire.

But this also is a futile **train of thought**.
For excessive power confuses the wise
And the intelligence is ruined by corruption.

Better is the end of the matter than its beginning
Better are the prudent than the arrogant.
Do not be in a hurry to become angry
For irrational anger is the monopoly of fools.

Do not say: How is it that the earlier days
Are better than now?
That is not a wise question you are asking.

Wisdom is better if accompanied by an inheritance.
An advantage to those who live to see the sun.
For as wisdom offers protection, so does wealth.
But the supremacy of knowledge is that
Wisdom can preserve the life of those who enjoy it.

Consider God's work
Who can make straight
What he has made crooked?
In prosperous times be happy
In bad times reflect
As God is the cause of one
So is he the cause of the other
And no person knows what will happen next.

I have experienced all things
In the days of my futile life.
The righteous who perish in spite of their virtue and
The wicked who live a long life in spite of there crimes.

Do not be over-righteous nor play the wise man.
Why do you want to alienate yourself **from others**?
Do not be too wicked nor too foolish.
Why should you court destruction before your time?

It is best to grasp the one
Without losing hold of the other
Because the God-fearing man will escape unscathed.[1]

Wisdom is a better fortress for the wise man
Than ten city magnates.
Do not trust in your righteousness
For there is not a righteous man on earth
Who only does good and never sins.

Do not be over-concerned with words said about you.
You may hear that your servant has condemned you
You yourself know how often you have
Thoughtlessly condemned others.

These guidelines I have discovered through my wisdom.
But when I said I will make myself truly wise,
It was beyond my reach.
The meaning of reality is so profound
Who is able to fathom it?

I turned myself and my mind in all directions
To learn and pursue wisdom and the reason of things
To study wickedness, stupidity, madness and folly.

I find more bitter than death is a woman
Who lures you into her trap
And her hands bind you up.
Only those favoured by God escape,
Sinners become her captives.

See this is what I have discovered, says Koheleth.
Adding one thing to another to come to some conclusion.
But that for which I was looking I did not find.

---

[1] The last three lines seem to suggest that the path of wisdom is to follow the golden rule of moderation, not to seek perfection but to take a pragmatic view of the best manner to proceed to achieve one's goals.

Only this that among a thousand I found one good man
But among all the women not even one.

This is my conclusion
God intended humans to be innocent
But they complicated their lives
By filling their heads with too many ideas.

*   *   *

Who is like the wise person
Who understands the meaning of the adage:
A person's wisdom lights up his face
He is able to hide his disdain?

I say: Obey the king's command.
Do not rush to swear by God's name
Give ground before him [the king]
Do not stand up for action he does not favour.
For he will do what pleases him.
For in the king's word is power
Who can question what he does?

Whoever keeps his orders
Will be spared evil times.
A wise man knows when
The time of judgement is coming.[1]

For there is a time for every matter to be judged
And the uncertainty of the human situation is a great
  evil.
He does not know what will happen
And even when it is about to happen
Who can tell him?

---

[1] Hebrew unclear. The context would indicate that a wise counsellor to the king has the discernment to know when he is about to lose favour at court.

No person has power to grasp the wind or
To keep the breath of life **within him**
No one has power over the day of his death
There is no defence in the war **against death**
Nor will wealth deliver its owner **from its clutches.**[1]

All this I have experienced
I have given all my attention
To every work performed under the sun
Especially when one man uses power to hurt another person.

I saw how the wicked were buried with honour
Those who used to parade in and out of holy places
How badly they behaved was forgotten.
But even this thought is futile.

Because sentence on a crime is not executed
The minds of human beings are prone to evil practices.
Even if a sinner acts wickedly a hundred times
And still prolongs his life
I still believe that it will be well
For those who fear God because they fear him.

The wicked will not enjoy prosperity
Nor a long life.
He will be like a shadow
Because he has no reverence for God.

What happens on earth is futile because
The righteous suffer as should the wicked
And the wicked prosper as should the righteous
But I thought that this too was a vain consideration.
So I praised joyousness

---

[1] The meaning of the last two lines is very unclear. Alternatively: You cannot send someone to take your place in a war to escape death, nor can wicked designs cheat the Angel of Death. 'Wealth' in place of 'wicked' is the result of an emendation in one of the texts.

For there is nothing better under the sun
Except eating and drinking and enjoying himself
That should be his comfort for his labour all
The years of his life which God has given him
Under the sun.

When I set my mind to learn wisdom
To see how people keep themselves busy on earth.
Keeping myself awake day and night
I observed all of God's work
But no one can comprehend
That which occurs under the sun.
No matter how much he perseveres in the quest
He will not find the answers
Even the wise philosopher who claims knowledge
Has no understanding **of the mysteries of life.**

*   *   *

To these efforts I dedicated myself
To clarify all these matters
The consequences of the works of the good and the wise
Are in the hands of God
Even in matters of love and hate
A person does not know to what they will lead.

All share one fate
The wise with the wicked
The pure and the impure
Those who offer up sacrifices and those who do not
The good as the sinners.
He who is quick to swear an oath and
He who is too cautious to do so.

This is what is so distressing
In all that happens under the sun
That all have one fate

Also that the sons of man are so inclined to evil
While they live they are filled with stupidity
And then they join the dead.

Still for those who are among the living there is hope
It is better to be a living dog than a dead lion.
The living at least know that they will die
The dead know nothing.
They do not even have any compensation
For the memory of them is lost.

Their loves, their hatreds
Even their envies perish
No longer have they any part in the world
In anything which happens under the sun.

So, go and eat your bread with joy
And drink your wine with a happy heart
For God wants you to enjoy the fruits of your labour.

Always dress in festive clothing
And spare no oil for your hair
Enjoy life with the woman you love
All the days of your vain life
Which has been given to you under the sun.

Yes, all your futile days
For that is your lot in life
And for all the work you perform
Under the sun.
Everything that you set your hand to
Do with all your strength
For there is no work
No reckoning
No knowledge and
No wisdom
In Sheol which is your destination.

I returned to my exploration of life
And realized that under the sun
The race is not to the swift
Nor the victory to the strong
Also that the wise can be without bread
And the clever without wealth
The geniuses can lack approval
All are subject to time and chance.

A person does not know his end
Like fishes caught in a treacherous net
Like birds trapped in a snare
So are the sons of men taken by surprise
When the evil moment suddenly falls upon them.

In this also did I learn wisdom under the sun
It impressed me very much
There was a small city with few people in it
Once a mighty king attacked it
He surrounded it and constructed
Huge siege works against it.
Now in that city was a poor but ingenious man
By his skill he saved the city
Yet nobody took any account of him afterwards.

So I concluded
While wisdom is greater than might
Still, the wisdom of the poor is despised
No one listens to his words.

The words of the wise spoken quietly
Are preferable to the shouting of kings among fools.
Wisdom is better than the weapons of war
But one evil sinner can wreak great destruction.

*   *   *

As dead flies make a perfumer's oil rancid
So a little stupidity **on his part** can
Ruin the respect for a man's wisdom.

A wise man's understanding
Guides him correctly.
A stupid man's understanding
Leads him astray.

Even when a stupid man is walking along
He loses discretion and proves himself a fool.

If a ruler's anger turns against you
Do not resign your post
For once his composure returns
Even serious offences can be pardoned.

A distressing matter have I experienced under the sun
That is through errors of judgment made by the ruler
Fools are advanced to high places
And men of substance relegated to lowly positions.
I have seen knaves on horseback
And noblemen walking as servants on foot.

He that digs a pit will fall into it
Whoever breaks through a wall will be bitten by a snake.
He who quarries stones may be hurt by them.
A wood chopper also endangers himself.

If the iron axe is blunt
And the edge not whetted
More strength will be needed
But skill gives greater advantage.

If the snake bites before it is charmed
The charmer has left it too late.
Just so the words of the wise win favour
But the lips of the fool lead to his ruin.

The words of his mouth begin with nonsense
But his final words are utter madness
Yet the fool talks on and on.

Ah, a person does not know what will be
Or what will happen after him
No one can tell him.

The work of fools wears them out
They do not know even how to follow directions into the
    city.
Woe unto you, O country
When your king is a boy
And whose officials revel in the morning
When there is work to be done.

Happy is the country
When your king is the master
And your officials revel at appropriate times
With control and not in a drunken state.

Through inattention the roof sinks
And through lazy hands the house leaks.

For laughter, have parties,
Let wine make life enjoyable
Money is the answer to everything.

Even in your thoughts
Do not condemn the king.
Even in the privacy of your bedroom
Do not condemn men of substance
For a bird in the air may carry the words
And a messenger may sprout wings
To report what you have said.

*   *   *

Cast your bread upon the waters
In time you will get it back again[1]
Make seven or eight portions **of your wealth**
For you cannot know what catastrophes can occur on
    earth.

All we know is that if the clouds are full of rain
Eventually they empty out on to the ground.
If a tree is struck down in the south or north
All we know is that in the place it falls there it will be.

He that watches the winds
Will never **think it the right time** to sow
He that worries about the rain clouds
Will never reap.

Just as you cannot know the ways of the wind
Or how bones grow in a pregnant belly,
Just so you cannot know how God works
Who is the maker of all things.

In the morning sow your seed
Even in the evening do not rest your hands,
For you cannot know what will prosper
This or the other or that both may be successful.

Light is sweet
It is a delight for the eyes to see sunlight
For if a person lives for many years
Let him seek joy in them all because
Let him remember the days of gloom
For there are many of them
And the future is futile.

---

[1] These images are designed to encourage investment in trade. You have to be
patient in waiting for a proper financial return. Also, hedge your investments.
Spread them about and keep a reserve.

Rejoice, young man, in your youth
Let your mind be positive when you are young.
Go after your heart's desires
And what your eyes fancy.

[But bear this in mind
That God will be the judge of all you do][1]
Banish all cares from your mind
and let your flesh be worry-free
For youth and a head of flowing black hair do not last.

*   *   *

Remember, then, your creator in the days of your youth
Before the evil days **of old age** come
And the years arrive when you will say
I take no pleasure in them.
Before the sun, the light and the moon
And the stars are darkened **by dimmed eyes**
Before the clouds appear to return after the rain.

When the guards of the house [arms] begin to tremble
And the strong men [legs] are bent
When the maids that grind [teeth] are few and lazy
And the ladies looking through the lattice [eyes] lose their
    lustre
When the doors [ears] to the street are shut
And the noise of the mill grows fainter
When one wakes up at the twitter of a bird
And the sounds of songs are barely audible.

Also, when going uphill is frightening
And terrors before every step in the way

[1] This warning goes against the whole tenor of Koheleth's advice. It may have been a pious insertion in order to achieve the book's admission into the Holy Canon.

When like the almond in blossom **the hair becomes white**
When like the grasshopper **the limbs shuffle along**
When the caperberry fails **to stimulate the appetite**
So does man walk the long road to his grave
While mourners go about in the streets.

Before the silver cord [the spine] snaps apart
And the golden lamp [the head] is shattered
And the pitcher [the stomach] is broken at the fountain
The broken pulley [the mouth] falls into the well
And the dust returns to the earth once more
And the breath of life returns to God who gave it.
Vanity of vanities, says Koheleth
All is utter futility.

It remains to be said that not only was Koheleth wise
But he continued to teach the people knowledge
He listened and examined and arranged many maxims.
Koheleth's aim was to create pleasing sayings
Well written and full of truth.

The sayings of the wise are like goads **to stimulate thought**
And like fixed pikes **which are difficult to contradict**
They are in a collection provided by one shepherd [Koheleth].
Beyond this, my disciples, be warned
There is no limit to the making of books
And too much study wears out the flesh.

To sum up
All things being considered,
Fear God and keep his commandments
This is the duty of all mankind
For every deed comes before God for judgement
Even everything hidden and secret
To determine whether it was good or evil.

The Book of Esther

The Book of Esther 1:1–11

My story begins during the reign of Xerxes, whose empire stretched from India unto Ethiopia. It encompassed one hundred and twenty-seven provinces. It was when the Emperor was sitting with his court in the citadel at Susa. During the third year of his rule he held a banquet for all his princes and officers and the warlords of the Medes and Persians. All the aristocracy and governors throughout his Empire were invited. He did this to show off the incredible wealth and splendour of his Empire and the majesty of his power.

The eating and drinking went on for days and days; some say for almost half a calendar year. **This was to enable no one to miss out for many would need months to travel the distances from the edges of the Empire**. To conclude the festivities, the Emperor invited all those who lived in the Citadel, commoners and grandees alike to enjoy a week's banqueting in the palace gardens. The guests were overwhelmed by the sheer luxury of the white- and blue-coloured drapes looped through silver rings to marble pillars with cords made of fine linen interwoven with purple threads. The couches had frames of gilt, gold and silver. The floors on which they rested were tiled in red, white, yellow and black marble. They drank from cups of gold, each designed with a different pattern. The wine was in great abundance as one would expect from the Emperor's cellars, but no one **on this occasion** was compelled to drink more than he wished for the Emperor had commanded his butlers to give the guests only what they required.

The Empress, Vashti, was also entertaining the women in her royal quarters. But on the very last day of the banqueting, when the Emperor was elated **by the impression he had made on his subjects and** by the amount of wine he had drunk, he ordered his seven valets to bring the Empress, Vashti, bedecked in her royal diadem to him to reveal her great beauty to his guests, and she had a most beautiful figure. **The valets made known to Vashti the Emperor's desire. She** asked after his welfare and through well-placed questions discovered that he was in a euphoric state, wishing to show her off before his entire party. **She told her ladies-in-waiting that she did not wish to go to be displayed before commoners.** Did he consider her but one more of his many possessions? **The valets begged her to heed the Emperor's demand as they feared for their own fate if they returned without her,** but the Empress refused to heed Xerxes's desire and this was reported to him by his valets.

The Emperor became mad with anger; his fury reaching boiling point. **How could she humiliate him on this the last day of the festivities and make a laughing stock of him and all his wealth and power?** As was the custom, the seven wisest men, known for their judgement of contemporary moods, were summoned to advise the Emperor. These counsellors were given unrestricted access to the Emperor and were virtually in charge of the empire. The question was put: "How to deal justly with Vashti for her refusal to obey the Imperial command?" Memuchan, one of the seven, made this sage declaration: "The Empress has not only wronged his Imperial Majesty, but the principle of authority itself, for her haughtiness has injured all men in authority, whether of aristocratic breeding or ordinary householders throughout the Empire. As soon as the women hear of the Empress's behaviour, they will be contemptuous of their husbands, for they will say, 'The Emperor ordered Vashti to come before him but she ignored his command.' So it will be that on this very day, **even while we speak**, the wives of all the distinguished men of Persia and Medea who have heard of her disobedience will treat them with equal contempt. This will lead to conflict and instability, **reaching even into the homes of your lowliest subjects**. Let the Emperor agree that a royal proclamation be made and to be considered as an irreversible edict and let it be publicly known throughout his domain that Vashti will never again see the face of the Emperor, but that he will give her royal dignity to a more deserving woman.

When this proclamation spreads throughout the empire, women will respect their menfolk of whatever station and position." **Xerxes and his counsellors were impressed by this reasoning.** So the Imperial order went out **that Vashti, the Empress adored by the Emperor, should never be seen by him again.** While it had **little significance to any of his subjects, nonetheless** dispatches of the banning of Vashti were distributed throughout all the countries of the Empire in every script and language so that **all would understand that** every man should be master in his household; **and, where there was an** intermarriage, the man's language would be spoken.

You will not be surprised however to hear that when the Emperor Xerxes **sobered up and** cooled down from his anger, he remembered **the charming ways of** Vashti and his irreversible decree **that he could never again see her.** But the young men who were the Emperor's men-in-waiting sought to console him. "Let the Emperor find comfort in the beauty of young virgins. All the Emperor needs to do is to appoint collectors in each of the kingdoms of his domain and let them bring together to his harem in Susa every girl who is both a virgin and beautiful, to be handed over to Hegay, the Eunuch-in-Chief. He will provide them with their oils and massages. And the lady who will give the Emperor most pleasure will rule his heart in the place of Vashti." The Emperor, **as you can imagine,** thought it a most appealing proposal, **and without consulting his counsellors** ordered its **immediate** execution.

At this time a Jew was living in the citadel at Susa. His name was Mordecai the son of Jair, the son of Shimei, the son of Kish from the tribe of Benjamin. They were those who along with Jeconah, the king of Judah, were forced into exile by King Nebuchadnezzar of Babylonia ... **He is important for our story.** He had a cousin who was exceedingly attractive. Both her parents having died, Mordecai became Esther's ward and he looked after her as one would a daughter. It was natural, therefore, when the King's decree was known and all the virginal beauties were being brought to Susa, Esther was, against her will, taken to the Court and handed over the Hegay, who was responsible for the Emperor's concubines. **Mordecai was desolated by her kidnapping but there was little he could do against the power of the Emperor.**

Hegay developed a soft spot for Esther and he was unusually kind to her. He gave her the most effective oils and best-smelling perfumes and whatever else she needed. He assigned her the most beautiful suite in the Emperor's harem and provided her with seven lovely hand-maidens from the palace. Esther, whose Hebrew name was Hadassah, did not let anyone know that she was Jewish or from what family she came, for Mordecai had advised her to keep this to herself. Every day Mordecai would loiter about the courtyard of the harem hoping that he would find out if Esther was well and what was happening to her. He **blamed himself for her captivity. He should have hidden her, for what would become of her as one of hundreds of the Emperor's concubines? After her night of trial in the Emperor's bed she would be shut away among chattering women whose lives were aimless, hoping that the Emperor might remember her name, so that she might for a night or part of it meet a man, who had not had his masculinity castrated. How badly he had betrayed the trust of his uncle who had felt confident in Mordecai's stewardship of his daughter's future. What also came to mind was the hope that one day he would have married his lovely cousin. She was younger than he but not by so many years to have made such a possibility obscene. Esther appeared to love Mordecai, for he was gentle and manly and handsome. She loved him as a brother, but that too could have changed when she matured and was no longer so dependent upon him. Imperial diktat prevented this romance from ever approaching fruition or even flowering. Still as Mordecai walked in the courtyard, hoping to catch sight of his Esther, he looked as much like a forlorn lover as he did an anxious cousin.**

In conversation with the eunuchs, he had learned the procedures facing his beloved Esther. Each of the girls would have

their turn to come before the king only after a year of preparation: six months for her to be pampered with the oil of the myrrh and a further six months with spices and perfumes. And, when the time came for her to come before the Emperor, whatever she asked was given her to accompany her from the House of Women to the palace of the Emperor. In the evening she would arrive, **entertain His Majesty** and in the morning she would return to the Second House of the Women under the charge of Sha-ashgaz, Keeper of the Emperor's Concubines. Her fate was never again to see the Emperor unless he yearned for her and remembered her name to summon her **to his bedchamber.**

The day drew near when Esther the daughter of Avihayil, whose nephew Mordecai had raised as a daughter, should appear before the Emperor. She asked for nothing and accepted whatever Hegay provided. **As Esther approached the Emperor's chambers, her seven maids held the tail of her gown.** Esther **in her modest but regal demeanour** won the praise of all, **the palace's courtiers and servants,** who laid eyes on her. **Even before he saw her, the Emperor had heard much about her and was awaiting her arrival with great anticipation. Would she be any different from the others in displaying her charms and affording pleasure to his jaded appetite?** So it was that Esther was brought to the Emperor Xerxes's royal rooms in the tenth month, Tevet, during the seventh year of his reign. **She bowed low before His Imperial Majesty. So stunned was he by her radiance that he stood up from the table laden with exotic fruit and delicacies of fish and meat, to take her hand and lead her to the sofa adjoining his own. He flicked his hand and all the maidens disappeared, moving backwards towards the draped entrance. Another Imperial gesture, and her cup of wine was filled and fruit was laid before her.** "Eat and drink, my child. Sustain yourself, it is my command!" **Esther bowed her head and took some pomegranate seeds which had been removed from their husks and raised them delicately to her mouth. As she ate them and as she drank the wine, the Emperor seemed mesmerised. Not once did her cup tremble as** she drank, nor did she look awkward as she swallowed the little morsels of fruit. "Are you not nervous before the great Emperor?" Xerxes chuckled as he said these words. "Should I be, my lord?" and she did not smile as she replied. "Come, come, it is not everyone who is alone with the Emperor." Esther did not reply until he insisted upon an answer. "No, my Lord, only those whom it pleases the king to see."

"Yes, and I am very pleased to see you. You are as beautiful as my servants said you were, but beauty is only skin deep, is it not, my child?"

"Yes, sir."

"I am told that you lived in Susa. But you have not revealed to anyone your origins or your ancestry. Tell me, my dear, who are you, who is your family and what is your history?"

"I am nothing but your servant, I have no family but the women and eunuchs in your harem, and my history begins now, and you are its author. My lord, press me no more."

"Beautifully spoken, but you tell me nothing. You think being a mystery will make you an even greater novelty for my pleasure?"

Esther lowered her head and allowed a blush to enter her cheeks and a slight tremor of her lips.

"Let it be as my lord wishes it."

"And how do you propose to give me pleasure, my girl?"

Esther did not reply. A few moments of silence passed until she heard the word, "Well?" from Xerxes's lips.

"I will do what the King requires."

"And no more?"

"Surely, doing what the Emperor demands must be enough?"

"But what of your own pleasure?"

"Your Majesty, I know nothing of the pleasures of which I think you speak. I am a virgin whose flesh has never been touched by a man. My pleasure will depend upon you. As you are my master, you will need to be my teacher, in receiving pleasure as well as giving it."

"How innocently you speak. This is a new challenge, I am to

become teacher! While you were in the Women's House, did you not enquire as to how you could best please me to win the crown?"

"I did not, my lord, for how could anyone but you know what in his heart of hearts pleases my lord. I chose not to hear the presumptions of others about your desires."

"Hmm, so you have no devices, no new ways of stroking or tickling or bodily movements to make me say, 'You shall be my Empress'?"

"No, my Lord, if beauty is skin deep, sexual pleasure must be only of a moment's duration."

"Now I have you! I thought you knew nothing of pleasure. So how do you know the length of its duration?"

"My mother, before she died, told me to marry the man with love in his eyes, for that would make me warmer than his body after it had its surfeit of sex."

"So, I must love you in order to give you pleasure?"

"No one can tell the Emperor what he must do. He will do what he wishes and he will have what he commands."

"Then I command that you love me."

"I want nothing more, my lord. Show me how."

With an unexpected motion she rose from her seat, went to the Emperor, bowed down, knelt, took his hand and kissed it.

That night, Xerxes taught her all he knew about the art of love. In giving delight, he had enjoyed delight he had not known. Esther was a grateful student, and expressed her gratitude with an innocence of youth. The Emperor felt young again and content. He slept that night like a child. Esther did not sleep but wondered if the art she had used to conceal art had won her the trophy of her master's heart and the royal crown.

The Emperor loved Esther more than any of the other women, for she was to him the quintessence of grace and gentility outshining all of the other virgins. And he placed the imperial crown upon her head, making her his empress in Vashti's place. The Emperor made a great feast for all his ministers. During Esther's coronation celebrations, he ordained a holiday throughout his kingdom, and he offered gifts with majestic generosity. Esther still did not reveal her origins or her people as Mordecai had advised. **Though she had now become Empress**, she still heeded his words just as she had when he was raising her.

Mordecai was still living in the grounds of the palace when the second group of virgins were assembled to be brought to the Emperor. **[Though Esther had been crowned, Xerxes saw no reason for sending back home the new arrivals. Touched as he was by Esther's love, the humanity she stirred in him existed for her alone. When they heard of the crowning of Esther they mourned for the loss of their lives, for they knew that all that remained for them was one night or part of it with the Emperor which would probably be their only one with him or any other man.]** It was during this time, when Mordecai was carrying out his business in the entrance to the Emperor's courtyard, that two of the Emperor's bodyguards, Bigtan and Teresh, who were stationed at the door of his inner chamber were upset and sought to injure the Emperor. Mordecai heard rumours to this affect and told them to Esther **because he believed that the story coming from him would not be believed.** She had it reported to the Emperor as coming from Mordecai. A thorough investigation found sufficient evidence to condemn the two conspirators to be hanged. This was all written down in the minute book in the presence of the Emperor.

After these happenings, the Emperor Xerxes elevated Haman, the son of Hammedata, the Agagite, and appointed him to such a high position that his seat in the council chamber was higher than the seats of all the other officers. **This caused Mordecai much distress for the tribe of Agag came from the nation of the Amalekites, who had since time immemorial been enemies of the Jews, and particularly of the tribe of Benjamin, to which Mordecai and Esther belonged. As far back as the exodus from Egypt, the Amalekites had in cowardly fashion slain the stragglers among the Israelites while they travelled through the wilderness. The Agagites especially hated the descendants of Benjamin because**

King Saul, a Benjamite, had almost wiped out the Amalekites when Agag, their ancestor, was king. So it was that, while all the ministers of the Emperor bowed before Haman, Mordecai would neither bend his knee to him nor prostrate himself before him. **No matter what the cost, he could not lose honour by showing obeisance to the enemy of his tribe and nation.** The Emperor's ministers remonstrated with Mordecai, "Why do you ignore the Emperor's order?" And, though they continually warned him **of his folly**, he paid them no attention. Some of them brought Mordecai's behaviour to Haman's attention to see if he would not stand up to him, **for in explaining his reason for not showing respect** Mordecai had told them that he was a Jew. **From that time forward, he was known as Mordecai the Jew.** Then Haman noticed that Mordecai did not bow nor prostate himself before him and became very incensed. But Haman thought it beneath his dignity to deal with Mordecai alone, for knowing of Mordecai's people, Haman would seek the destruction of all the Jews throughout Xerxes's empire for they were Mordecai's people.

It was on the first month of the year, which is Nisan, **the month of Israel's redemption from Egypt**, and in the twelfth year of Xerxes's reign, **five years after he made Esther his Empress,** that they cast the *pur*, lots, before Haman to find the most auspicious month **for the annihilation of the Jews. Finally,** the *pur* fell on the twelfth month, Adar. Haman made his request of Xerxes **with this introduction:** "There is a certain people scattered among all the nations but distinct from them in all the kingdoms of your Empire. Their laws are different from those of other nations, **but worse than this,** they do not keep the Emperor's laws and there is no reason for leaving them in peace. But, if the Emperor agrees to their destruction, ten thousand talents of silver [one billion pounds sterling] properly assayed will be deposited in the Imperial treasury." The Emperor removed the signet ring from his finger and handed it to Haman, the son of Hammedata, the Agagite, the persecutor of the Jews, and he said:

"Never mind the money, and do with this people whatever pleases you."

On the thirteenth day of the first month, the Imperial scribes were given their instructions. What Haman dictated to them was written and sent to all the governors of the provinces, the official heads of each district and all the **tribal** chieftains, each in their own language and script. As it was written and sealed with his signet ring, it had the authority of the Emperor. The couriers delivered the manifesto to each of his vassal states ordering the final destruction of all the Jews, young and old, mothers and babes **at their breasts**, all to be done on the same day, the thirteenth day of the twelfth month, Adar. All their possessions were to be taken as spoil. Instructions were also sent as to when the decree was to be publicized so that the populace could prepare for the appointed day of destruction, **but that the Jews should not have sufficient warning to make their escape or organize their defence**. The decree was first made known **at the Court** in Susa, while the Emperor and Haman were drinking together. **Knowing that something of great magnitude had happened but not knowing what,** those living in the City of Susa were in a state of confusion.

But Mordecai knew all that had happened **to the last detail between the Emperor and the arch villain, Haman. He could not control his grief and moreover he blamed himself for provoking Haman in this plan for his people's devastation. As is the custom among Jews in mourning,** he ripped his clothes, and covered himself with sackcloth and heaped ashes on his head. He went to the town centre and wept loudly and bitterly, **over the fate of his people.** So he went, shouting out the news, until he reached the Emperor's grounds. He could not enter its gates because his dress was improper. Whenever the contents of the Imperial command filtered through to the Jews in the provinces and districts, there was great mourning amongst them. The Jews fasted, wept and cried aloud. Many put on sackcloth and covered their heads with ashes.

Esther the Empress was shocked when her maidens and attendants told her of Mordecai's behaviour and dress. She had proper clothes delivered to Mordecai so that he might take off his sackcloth, but he rejected them. **Seeing how serious the matter was,** Esther sent Hatach, one of the Emperor's servants who attended her **and whom she could trust,** to her cousin to ask why he was in such deep mourning. Hatach found him on the main street of the city which was opposite the entrance to the Imperial palace compound. Mordecai told him what had happened, even the exact amount of silver that Haman had pledged to the Emperor for permission to destroy the Jews. He was also able to give him a copy of the decree which ordered their destruction which was **eventually** to be posted in Susa. He ordered her to approach the Emperor, to use her charms upon him and to seek her people's deliverance.

On hearing this message Hatach brought from Mordecai **and on reading the edict,** she told him exactly how to give her response to Mordecai. "**Say to him,** every minister knows, indeed everyone throughout the Empire knows that any person, male or female, who enters the Imperial inner chamber without permission is immediately killed unless the Emperor stretches forth his golden sceptre to spare him. Consider that I have not been summoned to the Emperor for almost thirty days. **This either means that he is now too involved with Haman's plans, but will soon call for me, which means I need take no risk, or that he has found out that I am a Jew and is not well disposed towards me, in which case my death is a certainty. Be patient, cousin, we have almost twelve months to thwart Haman's conspiracy against us and our people."** When Mordecai heard these words, **he peremptorily rejected them.** He sent back this message to Esther. "Do not think that, because you are part of the Imperial household, you will escape the fate of the Jews. Know that if you remain silent, **no matter what excuses you find for your silence,** a benefactor and deliverance for the Jews may come from another source, and you and your family name will be in disgrace. Consider whether it was not for this very reason, **and not your seductive power**, that you became Empress."

Esther heard these words from Hatach with sadness and deep hurt. How could her cousin Mordecai so completely misunderstand her motives! How could he have thought her so low that she would sacrifice her people, and her dear Mordecai, for her life of vanity and luxury at the Palace! What had happened to him? She would not argue, for who knows what he would do if she rejected his command. He might, in his present hysterical state of mind, inform the Court that, were Haman's plan to be implemented, the Empress would also die, as she too was Jewish, and this would be a catastrophe. She went into her inner bed-chamber, and prayed for guidance. **Within an hour**, she sent Hatach with these instructions for Mordecai: "Assemble all the Jews of Susa, and let them fast and pray for me. Let them not eat or drink until nightfall for three days. I and my maids, **however Imperial we are**, will also fast, and then I will approach the Emperor, notwithstanding the law against it, and if I perish, then I perish."

Esther's message filled Mordecai with remorse. He had projected his own guilt upon his dear Esther, and now she, at his command, was about to sacrifice her life for his own vanity before Haman. There was no going back now. On hearing her words, he proceeded to do as she had instructed. **So for three days the Jews of Susa, Esther and her maids fasted.** On the third day **of the fast**, Esther dressed in her regal gowns stood in the inner courtyard facing the Emperor's apartment. The Emperor was sitting in the Crown Hall with his face turned towards the entrance. When Xerxes saw Esther standing outside, he was pleased at the sight of her, and he held out the royal sceptre, and Esther approached until she touched the sceptre's head. And the Emperor questioned her. **"You have risked your life to see me, my Empress, my child.** What is your need, Esther, what is your wish? Ask up to half of the Empire, and you shall have it." Esther answered softly, "If it so please his Imperial grace, let the Emperor and

Haman come today to a meal I have made for him." The Emperor's face dropped. He stared into her eyes, wondering. "Still, my Esther is a mystery. I do not know where she comes from, and now she risks her life only to invite me and Haman to eat with her." Though he looked deeply into her eyes so that Esther could see that he was waiting to hear more, she said nothing. He broke the silence, "Off you go, my dear, to prepare our meal. I and Haman will be there." Esther smiled and withdrew. The Emperor gave instructions, "Tell Haman to come here immediately to fulfil Esther's desire."

That evening, the Emperor and Haman entered Esther's banqueting hall for the party she had prepared. "My lady," said Xerxes. "You look pale, are you not well?"

"No, my lord, I have been suffering from a heavy heart and my desire for food and drink has left me. So I wished to see you, for it has been long since you have called me. I knew that your favour and company would fill my soul with light and I would want to eat again and be merry in your presence. But, let us not talk about me, instead let us eat, drink and speak of whatever it is in the Emperor's heart to share with me of the affairs of state."

The conversation went from subject to subject. Esther had instructed the servants to keep the cups filled with wine. The quantity of drink loosened the lips of Haman, and Esther noticed the Emperor's dismay when he began to forget himself and offered answers to Esther's questions without his permission. It was then that the Emperor Xerxes asked Esther, "Now tell me what is your need and you shall have it, your wish, and it will be ours even up to half of the Empire." Esther answered: "This is my petition and this is my request," but before she continued she feigned faintness, begged forgiveness and continued, "I cannot tell my lord today, but if I please my lord and he wishes to hear of my petition and request, let the Emperor and Haman come tomorrow when, at the feast I will prepare for them, I will answer my lord's question." The Emperor agreed: "I can see that you are still not well. I shall leave you but will return tomorrow, and Haman will also accompany me if that is your wish, but tomorrow you must tell me what it is that is weighing on your mind."

While Xerxes left in a disturbed state, Haman was happy, almost euphoric, but when he saw Mordecai at the gates neither standing nor stirring before him, the insolence stuck in his throat. But Haman restrained himself until he came home. He called his advisors and Zeresh, his wife. He boasted of the glory that his wealth had achieved for him and of his many sons and of how the Emperor had lifted him up above all his nobility and ministers. "Not only this," Haman continued in full flow, "but the Empress Esther will not have the Emperor come to her banquets without me, and even tomorrow I have been invited to accompany Xerxes. But all this seems worthless so long as I keep on seeing Mordecai the Jew, **for that was how he had become known**, sitting disdainfully in the Emperor's compound." Zeresh his wife, and his friends and advisors were unanimously agreed: "Build a scaffold fifty yards high. Go to the Emperor early in the morning, ask his permission to hang Mordecai on it, so that by the time you arrive at the party with the Emperor, you will be in good cheer." Haman liked what they said and instructed the gallows to be built.

That night, the Emperor kept waking up, **for thoughts were flooding his mind which prevented an undisturbed sleep. What did his mysterious Empress want? Why would she not tell him immediately? Why the delay? And why had Haman to be present? She could not like that puffed-up moneybags. By the life of Marduk, I only put up with him because I need his money. Perhaps he has bought her too. Haman claimed that he knew nothing of Esther's reasons for the invitation. His arrogance is becoming insufferable. What is she up to? Does she think that Haman is needed to confirm my agreement to her petition, or are they in a joint conspiracy? With such thoughts, sleep continued to escape him until early morning. In the hope that the records of recent events might shed some light on the matter, he rose from his bed,** called for the minute books and had them read to him. They came to the record of Mordecai's accusation against Bigtan and Teresh's intrigue against the Emperor. On hearing this, the Emperor asked, "What great honour was given to Mordecai for saving my life?" The Emperor's lords-in-waiting had to confess: "He has received nothing at all." **The Emperor shouted, "By my life and the life of my ancestors, why should anyone tell me anything, if when they risk their lives for mine, they receive no acknowledgement, recognition or reward?"**

Still fuming with anger, he heard a rustling of feet and the clanging of swords. Who is out there? The Emperor's men told him, "It is Haman, **and his retinue."** "Order him to enter." When Haman came in, **and before he could utter a word,** the Emperor demanded of him, "What do you propose should be done for the man the Emperor desires to honour?" Haman could not help thinking, "Who would the Emperor want to honour more than me?" So he said, "Let the Emperor's royal apparel be brought, the very clothes the Emperor wears." **Xerxes thought: "So this is Haman's ambition," because he knew that Haman had himself in mind. Haman continued,** "And the royal steed upon which the Emperor rides and let the Imperial crown be put on his head and let the clothes and the steed be given to one of the Emperor's leading ministers and let him be the one to dress the man whom he desires to honour and let him be the man to lead the steed through the main thoroughfare of the city, crying out before him, 'Thus shall be done for the man whom the Emperor chooses to honour.'" **Shocked by Haman's overwhelming ambition, the thought struck him that Haman might want his Esther as well, as he would already have his crown and horse. It was with repressed pleasure that the Emperor instructed Haman,** "Be quick about it, take the clothes and the steed, just as you have said, and do all this for Mordecai the Jew who resides in my citadel. Do not dare leave out as much as one little detail of that which you advised!"

Mortified, Haman gathered together the clothes and the horse, **brought them to Mordecai's home** and personally dressed him

and placed him on the royal horse and led him through the main street, shouting and crying out before him, "This is what shall be done for the man whom the Emperor chooses to honour." **Mordecai was nonplussed. Had Esther done her work so successfully? He would not know until later as Haman would not speak to him. From his steed he looked on with amusement and raised his hand with gracious salutation as people bowed to him. Particularly pleasing was when he caught sight of those courtiers who had reprimanded him for not bowing before the very man who had become his runner and crier. When the main street had been traversed once and Haman led Mordecai back to his home to retrieve the clothes, the crown and the horse,** Mordecai then marched off to the gates of the Court, but Haman sought the refuge of his home, for his head was bowed low in despair and disgrace. Haman explained to his wife and friends all that he had suffered. **Word of his humiliation had already reached them for indeed some of them had witnessed it. They turned his words over in their heads, especially that of his meeting with the Emperor. They could offer no words of comfort, for they felt the tables had been turned. Haman had reached his zenith and now he would fall to the ground.** With one voice, his counsellors and wife Zeresh said, "If it is before Mordecai, a descendant of the Jews, that you have begun to fall, you will never succeed against him, because you will be crushed by him." As they were still speaking to him, the Emperor's attendants arrived to rush Haman off to Esther's supper. **He had no time even to remove the dust from his clothes and sandals.**

So both the Emperor and Haman arrived together to drink and eat with Esther the Empress. **Both they and Esther were anxious but for different reasons. As soon as the courtesies after the first drink and bites of food were done,** while drinking **a toast to Esther,** the Emperor asked Esther, **as politely as he had done before,** "What is your petition and it will be granted, and what your desire, even unto half the Empire, it shall be yours." **Esther jumped to her feet, then fell on her knees, grasped the Emperor's legs,**

putting her face on his knees. He removed her face with his hands. Esther said to him softly, "If the Emperor loves me and if it pleases my lord, my petition is only for my life and my desire for the deliverance of my people because both I and my people have been sold for death and destruction." Before the Emperor could interrupt her words, she rushed on headlong. "If we had been only sold to be slaves and handmaids, I would have been silent for I would not have wanted to limit any profit my enemy would bring to the Emperor's business."

The Emperor Xerxes asked Esther, "Who is the man and where is he who has it in his heart to do this?" And Esther, **rising to her feet, and returning to her lounging sofa,** said, "My adversary and my enemy is this wretched Haman!" And Haman quaked before the Emperor and Empress. **The Emperor heard this accusation with a mixture of relief and guilt. All was now clear to him, Esther herself was Jewish, and it was he who had conspired with Haman to wipe her people out. Esther was totally innocent, what a relief! Haman and he were the guilty parties – Haman the villain, and he the greedy fool.** With feigned uncontrollable anger the Emperor withdrew into the garden **to decide on the best course of action to extricate himself from Haman and his own collusion in the destruction of the Jews. Haman did not pursue the Emperor because he knew that he had chosen Esther over him.** Convinced that the Emperor was now determining how to punish him, he stood up to plead for his life from Esther the Empress. When the Emperor returned from the garden into the banqueting room, he found Haman had fallen upon Esther's couch. **This was the excuse he needed.** "Will he even ravish the Empress while I am in the house!" As soon as his words were heard, the guards put a cover over Haman's face as was the custom when a man's fate was doomed by the Emperor. Harbona, an attendant of the Emperor, **seeing that the time was ripe** told him: "Haman has built gallows exceedingly high for Mordecai, the man who spoke for his majesty's welfare. It is in his grounds." The Emperor bellowed, "Hang him on it." So it happened that Haman was hanged on the gallows he had intended for Mordecai. And the Emperor's anger subsided.

When Haman was taken away, the great Xerxes took Esther and had her sit by him on the couch. He confessed that he had agreed the destruction of the Jews, and were it not for her it would have been executed. He admitted also his suspicions of her relationship with Haman, and his relief that he had misjudged her. To make amends, the estate and wealth of Haman, because of his persecution of the Jews, would be given to her. Then Esther told him of Mordecai's relationship to her. Surprised but pleased, he instructed that Mordecai be brought to the Emperor. At Esther's suggestion, Xerxes agreed that Mordecai should take control of Haman's estate on her behalf and his, for did not all she owned belong to him! The Emperor accordingly removed the signet ring which had been taken from Haman and gave it to Mordecai so that he and Esther had the power to confiscate Haman's estate. The Emperor parted from Esther and Mordecai, after advising her that he would be asking for her company that evening. Mordecai asked Esther about all that had happened and she told him with great glee how she had succeeded in winning the heart of the Emperor. He joined in her excitement, for now both had wealth and power beyond their dreams: "But what of the edict against the Jews? We are saved, but what of our brothers and sisters, you must speak of them tonight when you see the Emperor." Full of confidence, Esther said that she would not discuss it with him that evening. That night, she said, would be devoted to his pleasure. Mordecai winced at the thought but remained silent. Esther had taken command of the situation. She was no longer his cousin. She had become his Empress. The Emperor and Empress spent a night of eating, drinking, music and love-making. No words of business or the day's events passed their lips, though both made fun of the sudden end of Haman's rise to power. Esther withdrew to her own chambers before he awoke.

In the morning the Emperor was deeply involved in handing

over to his other ministers all the business of the Empire which Haman had supervised. They were told that Haman's estate had been confiscated and given to Esther with Mordecai as manager of his properties and businesses. These affairs of state were interrupted when the Emperor and his ministers saw the Empress approach the Emperor and fall at his feet. He touched her head with the golden sceptre. She did not stand but on her knees said, "I have been selfish. I have been satisfied with the downfall of my enemy, Haman, and have accepted my Lord's generosity of his wealth, but I have done nothing for my people who are condemned by Imperial decree to be massacred on the Thirteenth Day of Adar." And thus, she begged him to reverse the evil which Haman, the Agagite, had conspired to commit against the Jews. She stood up before the Emperor, saying in a pleading voice: "If the Emperor feels favourably towards me and loves me and feels it appropriate and also believes that I only want his welfare, let him repeal all the edicts conceived by Haman, the son of Hammedata the Agagite, which prescribed the annihilation of all the Jews living in all parts of the Empire." The Emperor took her hand and patted it. "This is not for you to deal with, my lady, we will send for Mordecai and together resolve the matter." When he arrived and prostrated himself before the Emperor, Xerxes said to Esther and Mordecai, "Know that you have my favour, I have already given over to Esther Haman's estate, and he has been hanged because he threatened not only you but the Jews. But you must know that whatever has been sent out by royal decree cannot be annulled. You have my authority to make any decree concerning the Jews which pleases you. Do it in my name and seal it with the royal signet ring."

So, on the twenty-third day of the third month, Sivan, they summoned the Imperial Scribes. What they wrote in accordance to Mordecai's dictation was dispatched to the Jews, the district officials, the **tribal** chieftains and the governors of the provinces extending from India to Ethiopia, all in all one hundred and twenty-seven provinces. It was written for each province in its own script and in the language of each people, and in the same manner it was written to the Jews, **as they were widely dispersed through the Empire and spoke the language of their host peoples**. All the edicts had the authority of Xerxes confirmed by his Imperial seal. The missives were delivered by couriers on the swiftest steeds from the royal stables. It gave permission for the Jews in each town and village to assemble and stand up for their lives, to crush, kill and destroy the forces of their enemies and to take their women, children and possessions as spoil. All this was to be done on one day throughout the provinces of the Empire, **the very day chosen by Haman for the destruction of the Jews**, the thirteenth day of the twelfth month, Adar.

Copies of a summary of the proclamation sent to all the provinces were posted for all the people to see, that the Jews should muster themselves for the day when they would rid themselves of all their enemies. While the couriers on their swift steeds went off in haste, as a matter of urgency as it was by Imperial command, the decree was immediately posted in the citadel at Susa. **At the time of its posting**, Mordecai was seen to be leaving the Emperor's chambers in clothes of royal colours and on his head an official headdress gilded in gold, and wearing a fine purple linen gown, **for the Emperor had heaped honours on him as he had once done for Haman.** The city of Susa rejoiced **at the fall of Haman and rise of Mordecai.** But, especially, the Jews were glad and exhilarated by their deliverance and the new dignity given to them. In every province and every town – every place where the Imperial edict reached – the Jews were overwhelmed with joy. They declared holidays and organised parties. Many common folk converted out of fear for the new power given to the Jews.

Finally, the thirteenth day of the twelfth month arrived, the day for the execution of the Imperial decree when the Jews were to break the yoke of their enemy and to reverse their situation, in so far as to have the upper hand over those who hated them. The Jews mustered their strength in every city of the Emperor's domain to strike out against those who wished them harm. No man dared stand in their way, for all were frightened of them. The provincial officials, high commissioners, governors, local chieftains, all the Emperor's civil servants showed respect to the Jews because they were in fear of Mordecai's standing, for the influence of Mordecai in the Imperial Court continued to grow and knowledge of this became widespread in all the provinces and everyone spoke of his increasing power. So, the Jews were able to deal a decisive blow against their enemies. Their swords struck out and slew for they were able to do whatever they wanted against those who hated them. In Susa, the citadel, the Jews killed five hundred men. They also killed the ten sons of Haman, the son of Hammedata, persecutor of the Jews. But they refrained from laying their hands on their women, children or possessions, **even though they had royal permission to do so.**

The tally of the dead in Susa was told to the Emperor. He was speaking to Esther the Empress **[who in the course of the months before the day of reckoning had taken a greater interest in the affairs of the Empire, and often sat next to him in the Crown Room]**. "I hear that in Susa the Jews have killed five hundred men and the ten sons of Haman. What havoc have they wreaked in the rest of my Empire?" **Esther said that she had no news. Detecting that her master felt that he was losing control of the situation, she fell at his feet and asked: "Have I done anything to lose my lord's favour? Have I and Mordecai gone beyond the Emperor's command in killing so many of our enemies?"** But he, **quickly mollified, replied, "Not at all, my love,** whatever you want, it is yours, whatever you ask, it shall be done." Esther then made this request **teasingly as if to test him:** "Well, if I have found favour let the Jews have also tomorrow to fulfil the royal decree, and also I would like the bodies of Haman's sons to be hung on gallows **to be a deterrent to others who would seek to harm any of the Emperor's loyal subjects.**" The Emperor ordered it done. An extension of the decree for another day was posted and the sons of Haman were exposed on the gallows, **for all to see.** The Jews of Susa assembled again on the fourteenth day of Adar and killed a further three hundred men but again took no booty. The Jews who lived in the other provinces of the Empire mustered their forces to defend themselves, finally to have rest from their enemies and they killed from among those who hated them seventy-five thousand. But they too took no spoil, **nor laid a hand on the wives and children of their enemies.**

This happening **in the provinces** on the thirteenth day of Adar, they rested on the fourteenth day of the month, held parties and enjoyed themselves. The Jews in Susa, however, having fought both on the thirteenth and fourteenth made their holiday on the fifteenth when they had their celebrations and parties. It is for this reason that Jews who are scattered in different cities celebrate the fourteenth day of Adar as a holiday for parties and merriment and the exchange of presents among family and friends.

Mordecai recorded these events, **which I have described,** and sent letters to all the Jews who were in the provinces of the Emperor, Xerxes, both near and far to institute the fourteenth and fifteenth days of Adar as an annual holiday, a day for giving of presents to one's loved ones and charity to the poor. **He did this because,** in those days, the Jews were granted respite from their enemies, for in that month their fortunes had changed, from anxiety to relief, from mourning to festivities. And the Jews were happy to carry on the custom as Mordecai had ordered in his letter. For it was quite extraordinary that Haman the son of Hammedata, the Agagite, the perennial adversary of the Jews, devised to wipe out the Jews and cast *purs* to find the most felicitous time for their destruction, but when the matter was concluded by the Emperor, decrees were issued which turned his plans upside down to the point that it was he, **and not Mordecai,** and his sons who were hanged and exposed on the gallows. So it was that those days of festivities became known as Purim because of the pur **which was cast before Haman.** As a result of a further letter and their own experience of these events, the Jews were happy to accept and institute for themselves and their children and their descendants not to fail in the observance of these two days as the letter had prescribed and to do so year by year on the given dates. These days would be remembered and observed by every family in every nation, in every city from generation to generation, so that the days of Purim would always be commemorated by the Jews and that the Festival would never cease to be a day of remembrance for their descendants.

Of course, the proclamation of the second letter **of instruction** was made with the force of the authority of the Empress Esther, the daughter of Avihayil, and Mordecai the Jew. And he sent these letters to all the Jews living in the one hundred and twenty-seven provinces of Xerxes's Empire. With sincere wishes for their welfare, they were asked to establish the days of Purim in their time as Mordecai the Jew and Esther the Empress had requested of them and future generations, and also to commemorate through annual fasting **her fast and that of the Jews of Susa before she went before the Emperor.**

And when it came to the attention of Mordecai the Jew, that the treasury of the Emperor had not received the promised ten thousand talents of silver pledged by Haman which he meant to achieve through the confiscation of their wealth following their destruction, and that the Emperor had need of this money, Mordecai levied taxes on behalf of the Emperor on the entire mainland and the isles of the surrounding seas. **This is but one of his services rendered to the Emperor.** But all the acts revealing Mordecai's might and power and the greatness bestowed upon him by the Emperor are **said to be** inscribed in the annals of Persia and Media. For Mordecai the Jew was second to the Emperor Xerxes and greatly honoured among the Jews and loved by most of his kinsmen because he sought their welfare and spoke gently to them and their children. **And this was his comfort as he saw his beloved, Esther, whom he had hoped to make his wife, loved and honoured by His Majesty, the Emperor Xerxes.**

Epilogue to The Book of Esther

The Book of Esther is a well written farce. There is no evidence of any historical basis for the account. There may have been times when the Jews were rescued from their persecutors by co-religionists and this could be the kernel of this elaborate tale. Of all the books of the Bible this is the only one in which God is not mentioned. While there are other reasons given to explain this, the most plausible is that the author had too much respect for God to make of him a character in a fictional narrative; he was too pious to take the name of God in vain. Modern readers must also appreciate that the writer would have had no idea that, centuries after it was written, there would have been a collection of books called the Bible and that the ancient rabbis would have seen fit to put this book into a Holy Canon.

The author would have maintained, and this was the view of the audience, that if the events did not happen, they should have! The popularity of the book was guaranteed by the artful interweaving of issues of life and death with the toings and froings of a comical villain, a beautiful heroine and an egocentric emperor. Circumstances are invented which by necessity lead to the defeat of a hapless villain and the exaltation of the intended victim. Sober sentiments and diabolically clever arguments are juxtaposed with scenes filled with comedy and suspense.

Fictitious or not, the events described in *Esther* became the occasion for the Jewish Festival of Purim which is celebrated on the date when Haman intended to wipe out all the Jews in the Persian Empire but which date, due to the intercession of Esther, became a day of Jewish victory and triumph. On Purim, *Esther* is read publicly in Synagogues. Feet are stamped, noisemakers clatter, there are jeers and hoots each time the arch-villain's name is mentioned.

The Defeat of Anti-semitism

As anti-semitism has been a disease infecting the world for over two thousand years, the book has never lost its relevance. Because of this, the fact that there is no historical evidence for the book has not diminished its popularity. It is thought to have been written when the Jews were suffering under the foreign oppression of Antiochus IV and before their successful rebellion under the Maccabeans (c. 165 BCE). Its intention was to tell a good story which would inspire the Jews to believe in their ultimate triumph over their enemies. While it is the Jews who enjoy deliverance in the story, its relevance is not limited to them. Irrational hatred destroys the foundations of society, which are tolerance and trust.

Xerxes and Vashti

The scene is set in Susa, the opulent capital of the Persian Empire. The time is any period from the 6th century BCE to Alexander's conquest of Persia in the second half of the 4th century. The Emperor Xerxes [in Hebrew, *Ahasuerus*], to show off his wealth and power, gives a party lasting 180 days for all the dignitaries of his realm. As a climax, he invites all the citizens of Susa to a seven-day feast. Xerxes is satisfied that the populace is sufficiently impressed. But on the last day of the party when he is drunk on wine, he decides to show off his beautiful wife. The Queen takes offence at the Emperor's wish to make her into a spectacle for a carousing rabble of commoners. Xerxes is mortified by her refusal which became public knowledge. Thus, in a moment of pique, the Queen demolishes the entire objective of six months to celebrate the Emperor's glory. Xerxes is drunk with rage and his discomfiture is elevated into a great matter of State. If Vashti's impertinence is allowed to go unpunished, Persian society will be turned upside down. Women will cease to obey and respect their husbands throughout the Empire. Vashti must be put away and another made Queen in her place.

Mordecai and Esther

Xerxes regains his sobriety, and recalls with fondness the beautiful Vashti and the edict against her which according to Persian custom even he cannot revoke. His friends come up with a solution to take his mind off the lovely Vashti. Virgins are to be collected from all parts of the Empire, and after a year's preparation to be taken to the Emperor's bed. A "great number of girls were brought to the citadel of Susa" for this purpose. As the Emperor already possessed many concubines, the size of his harem would have increased enormously; so it was likely that certain ladies of the harem would never see the Emperor more than once during their lifetime.

Esther, cousin and adopted child of Mordecai who lives in the palace grounds, is among the girls brought to the Emperor. She wins his favour and is crowned Empress. She heeds her cousin's advice not to inform anyone of her Jewishness. Her ability to conceal her identity indicates that she was an assimilated Jewess. Both she and her cousin are named after Babylonian deities, Ishtar (Astarte) and Marduk. (To name a Jewish child Christopher would be today's equivalent to naming a child Mordecai in Persia.)

Haman the Amalekite

It is significant that Haman, the villain of the piece, is from the land of Agag. There is no country known by this name, but this is the name of the king of the Amalekites whom Saul, the first king of Israel, defeated in battle. The nation of Amalek, according to the Bible, was the arch enemy of the Israelites and the symbol for human evil. Their primal crime was to attack the stragglers in the Israelite march from Egypt to the Promised Land. For this cruelty towards the weak and defenceless, God had commanded the Israelites to blot out even the memory of Amalek. *"Remember what Amalek did to you on the journey after you left Egypt – how, unafraid of God, he ambushed you when you were famished and weary, and cut down those who were faint in the rear. Therefore when The Lord, your God, grants you safety from all your enemies around you, in the land that The Lord, your God, is giving you as an inheritance, you shall blot out the memory of Amalek from heaven. Do not forget!"* [Deuteronomy 25:17–19]. Thus Moses declares: *"The Lord will be at war with Amalek throughout the ages."* [Exodus 17:16] Amalek, Agag and Haman are personifications of the evil which must be uprooted from civilization. Mordecai and Esther are from the tribe of Benjamin, as was King Saul who fought the Holy War against Amalek. The battle of Mordecai and Esther against Haman becomes a metaphor for the perennial fight between Israel and Amalek, and the struggle between the godly and the satanic.

Haman's Hatred

Haman, having been appointed Grand Vizier, had a justified complaint against Mordecai for not bowing to him in accordance with the Imperial order. Discovering that Mordecai is a Jew, he decided to feed his hatred's greed by destroying the entire Jewish people. His reason for demanding the destruction of the entire people, children as well as men and women, is the justification of every bigot: the fear of the unknown: *They are different and their ways are different.* Haman knew that his argument against the Jews was irrational and therefore offered Xerxes a bribe of 10,000 talents of silver. The motive of material gain is still a common means for turning one group against another.

Esther Risks her Life

Esther's desire to delay going to the Emperor to plead for the life of her people, though justified by her, gives the author, through Mordecai, the opportunity to warn people not to think that they will escape persecution because of their elevated positions in society.

Esther proves to be a clever diplomat. Her life being spared, she delayed in making known her real petition. Had she informed the

Emperor that her life was threatened because she was Jewish, Haman could well have accused her of not having revealed her identity sooner, thus fortifying Haman's argument that the Jews were not a people to be trusted and a danger to the stability of the nation. She creates suspicion of Haman in the mind of Xerxes. What follows is a series of scenes which comically lead to Haman being brought down from his dizzy heights to be raised again on the gallows built for Mordecai.

The Elevation of Mordecai

The conclusion is happy. The relationship of Mordecai and Esther is made known. Mordecai is given the wealth and position of Haman. While the Emperor cannot revoke his edict against the Jews, a new decree gives them "the right to assemble in self-defence, with permission to destroy any people or province that might attack them . . ." This the Jews successfully do. They refrain from taking the plunder of battle, though they have permission to do so. Mordecai sends letters to Jews in all the provinces of Xerxes to institute the annual festival of Purim on the day in which according to the *pur* which Haman has cast, the Jews were to have been destroyed but which day became for them instead a day of victory.